My Story
His Glory

Contact information for His Glory Publishing– contact@hisglorypublishing.com

ISBN: 978-0-9651007-4-8 (paperback)
ISBN: 978-0-9651007-5-5 (ebook)
ISBN: 978-0-9651007-6-2 (hardcover)
ISBN: 978-0-9651007-7-9 (audiobook)

Ordering Information:
Special discounts are available on quantity purchases by corporations, associations, and others. For details, contact— contact@hisglorypublishing.com

My Story
His Glory

A Lens on Racism and Religion in America
and God's Final Judgment

Understanding
The Angels of Revelation Series

Book 1

Nathaniel X. Arnold

Dedicated to my God, my family, and my friends.

Contents

Foreword

O ver the past several years, I have had the privilege of knowing Nathaniel Xavier Arnold as his pastor, brother, and friend. During that time, I have been repeatedly enriched by his benevolent spirit, buoyant faith, refreshing authenticity, and radiant passion for the word of God. It has been truly heartening to observe him blossom in his faith—even while enduring a multitude of experiences including personal tragedy and loss.

Additionally, as one of the ordained elders of our congregation, Nathaniel has been a consistent model of one who selflessly gives his time and resources toward building up the kingdom of God, without complaining or wanting reward. A true warrior for Christ, he regularly shares with others how the power of God changed him and set him free from the chains of sin, anger, and unbelief. I am convinced that it is out of his sense of gratitude to God and his commitment to sharing truth, especially relevant to these times, that this volume was birthed.

My Story, His Glory is a multi-layered, riveting account of Nathaniel's life and journey of faith. He skillfully recounts details of his rich life through the lens of an African American male born in the segregated south, who then matriculates to Washington, D.C. It is the sacred telling of a rare narrative that blends and chronicles his personal stories of racism and discrimination (which was and is so prevalent within the church and society), while trying to grapple with the relevance of the Bible, and in particular, its prophecies. His commitment to honesty and transparency in this volume is particularly noteworthy, especially in this digital age of carefully guarded posts that seek to relay images of perfection.

This book begins at his childhood, within the confines of a Christian home. He ultimately moves on to share the time, when, after ceasing to actively practice Christianity, he began an extensive search of the deeper meaning of life within the portals of Pan-Africanism. Nathaniel asserts that this pivotal decision was made because of the frustration, bitterness, and anger that resided within his soul after discovering the glaring contradictions between what Christianity teaches, as opposed to what its adherents practice—particularly, the prominent and blatant racism that exists within every level of society and even within the Christian church, often in the name of Christ. It was during this period that Nathaniel penned the critically acclaimed book, *The Genocide Files*.

However, I am glad that his story does not end there. After much prayer, struggle, and research, Nathaniel shares the details of his slow journey back to Jesus and how he regained his footing and purpose within the poignant message of the "sanctuary" that is found in the scriptures. From that study, he realized that the root cause of every type of wickedness, evil, and brokenness found in humanity is because of sin. He also discovered that the only antidote to all sin and its manifestations is found in a relationship with Jesus.

Finally, this dedicated author offers a direct challenge to professed Christian and non-Christians alike to wake up and begin to view each of our lives in light of Biblical prophecy because we may well be living in the last days. He asserts that it is time to examine our lives personally and corporately in the hope that it will ultimately lead all to confess Jesus Christ as Lord, as well as revealing whatever sins must be removed before the church can truly experience the full outpouring of the Holy Spirit, which God has promised.

My Story, His Glory is indeed a fresh telling of the greatest story ever told with a socially relevant backdrop. It is a message told with love, yet without apology. I believe it will truly impact your life as well as your eternity.

—Dr. Emil D. Peeler

The Lord Is My Shepherd

✝ *David said moreover, The LORD that delivered me out of the paw of the lion, and out of the paw of the bear, he will deliver me out of the hand of this Philistine, And Saul said unto David, Go, and the LORD be with thee.*

—I SAMUEL 17:37 KJV

A**s a child, one of my earliest** memories is of a beautiful, early spring morning. I am not sure of the year or my exact age. I don't remember the faces or the names of the children there with me on that easy Easter Sunday morning. I do remember that we were dressed in our best Sunday go-to-church clothes and that the adults were extra attentive as they sat us on the side front row of the church. They left us with firm instructions to be still and pay attention to the preacher and the deaconesses.

As I sat there waiting, my excitement was barely manageable. It was nearly impossible for me not to talk to the other children who were sitting in our row, but we had been given our instructions. Still, I fidgeted relentlessly. In the days before, I had spent what seemed like an eternity memorizing the verses to the 23rd Psalm. I wasn't sure what all the words meant, but they must have been important. "The Lord is my Shepherd" (v. 1). I knew that King David had written that psalm and that he was talking to God when he did. I knew that they had a special relationship.

David and Samson were my favorite people in the Bible. Samson was strong, like I wanted to be. And David—well, David was brave, and he killed Goliath! David and Samson were my heroes. I wanted to be strong and brave just like them. They both talked to God and God talked to them. I knew God, too, but maybe not in the same way they did. I was just a little boy, nothing special about me. God had never talked to me or chosen me to slay lions or giants.

As a child, my heroes were real to me, I had seen them on the small screen, and I knew God was real even though I couldn't see Him. I learned to pray early in life. Now I prayed that I would get the words to the psalm right. It was important to my mom, and to Papa and Mama, my grandparents, who were all there watching me. God answered my prayer as He always had. I recited the verses flawlessly, as all the "Amens" from the adults in church attested.

A few short years later, I was confused as I sat alone, squarely in front of the black and white television in my grandparents' home at 252 South Cedar Street in Mobile, Alabama. I knew something was wrong with the world, but I did not quite understand what exactly it was. The wrong was what stirred the confusion in my young mind. There was a lot of anger and fear all over the country, and it poured out right into my living room through the television. Alabama seemed to be the center of the world, and it seemed, every night we were on the news. Governor Wallace and the police were trying to stop Black people, people like me, from marching and protesting. The police were hurting some of them and killing others. They used fire hoses and German Shepherd dogs against unarmed men and women. That was wrong and President Kennedy seemed to feel that way, too. He sent soldiers against Wallace and the police. At almost seven-years-old, it didn't make sense to me. The world seemed unfair, and that made me angry.

I sat there by myself wondering, with a child's inquisitive mind and super-ficial understanding, when a hair commercial interrupted my reverie. The White woman whisked her long, flowing hair from side to side to accen-tuate it as White women so often do. I marveled at it and her beautiful, rehearsed elegance.

Then, abruptly, that picture was replaced by the angry and calculated words of Governor Wallace as he stood in front of the cameras at the Uni-versity of Alabama, forbidding the entrance of two students, both Black like me. "Segregation now, segregation tomorrow, segregation forever," were the words still ringing from Wallace's inauguration speech made a few months before. As I watched Vivian Malone, who lived in my home-town of Mobile, and James Hood stand in regal silence before the racist demagogue, the image was branded into my young consciousness. The juxtaposition of those two images, the picture of White beauty and the rage at Blackness, deepened the confusion surrounding my world and coupled it with a tinge of sadness that would haunt the remnant of my childhood innocence.

Kennedy and Wallace were both White men of authority. One seemed to like Black people, the other one didn't. Why? Who was right and who was wrong? What had we done as Black people? Were we bad? Were we evil? Was I bad? I thought God loved everybody. The television was full of those same contradictions. Why were there no Black people, people that looked like me, on my favorite shows—*Bonanza, Wanted: Dead or Alive, and Walt Disney's Wonderful World of Color*? Disney was especially perplexing because of its absence of color!

My puzzlement grew and it became unbearable. I sat there mesmerized, compelled to watch, as Vivian Malone and James Hood with their protective brigade of soldiers walked past the mob of angry White people and past the governor, into the school building. Fixed on the scene unfolding before me, I thought silently to God and questioned Him. "Why did you make me a Negro?"

The Presence of God

I knew from my young experience that God loved me. I can't explain how I knew, but I knew. I remember having to get regular shots for a liver or blood ailment I had as a small child, which made my stomach swell. My Aunt Annie Mae would walk me from my home to the doctor's office, weekly for about 30 weeks. I would always take my time, commenting and touching every flower or unique plant along our route. She never rushed me. She knew that the shot in my arm waiting for me at the doctor's office was something I hated. I always cried bountiful tears until I got the lollipop for being a "good boy" when it was over.

There was one other thing I remember about those long walks: It was the presence of God. I felt a peace and serenity that I couldn't put a name to, yet it was real, and it was precious. I knew that the sharp pain in my future would soon pass away and that I would be alright. Maybe that was because of Psalm 23.

Yea, though I walk through the valley of the shadow of death, I will fear no evil: for thou art with me; thy rod and thy staff they comfort me (v. 4).

Annie Mae's patience with me is an example of how God is with us, only more so. As a child, I did not understand His patience, but it was a reality, nonetheless. That question I posed to God all those years ago; He answered for me, not how I thought He would, but in a way that demonstrated His love and the power of His promises. This book is about His promises and His love. You may not have exactly the same questions I had, but I guarantee you, God has the answers.

My Story. In the Valley of the Shadow

This is my story; an intimate and sometimes painful revealing of my journey—conversion, fall, and restoration. It is my testimony, but none of it would be possible without the greatest of gifts given by the greatest of Givers, the sacrifice of Jesus Christ the Righteous. It is all to His glory that I write this book. My purpose in writing is to encourage, enlighten, and help those ensnared, just as I was, by the enemy of souls in this most critical of times. The "end time" deceptions are pervasive, subtle, and diabolical. If it were possible, even the very elect would be deceived (see Matthew 24:24).

Although my personal story spans not even a full 65 years, the experiences and revelations I will discuss encompass the nearly 6,000 years of earth's history, from God's creation of our world in six literal days to the fast-approaching "Day of the Lord" that we have termed "the last days." If all of this seems strange to you, I pray that by the end of *My Story, His Glory*, it will make much more sense.

The writing of this book was not intentional, at least not on my part. I was going through a life crisis. I had just been diagnosed with cancer for the second time in my adult life. My younger brother had died less than a year before, and I was not sure if God loved me and if I could trust Him. That was a terrifying thought. Fortunately, I learned the necessity of prayer in trying and uncertain circumstances. It is when you have doubts and perplexities that you need to talk to God the most. As the Apostle Peter wrote, "Give all your worries and cares to God, for He cares about you" (1 Peter 5:7 NLT).

So, on an early and rainy weekday morning, I found myself sitting in my car overlooking the water at a scenic vista in Fort Washington Park. I was wondering about God's plan for me, if I would live or if I would die. The misty rain falling so gently on my windshield matched my mood exactly. My mind ran back and forth between a thousand yesterdays filled with memories both pleasant and unpleasant. None of it made much sense, as I listened to the silence of the morning whispering doubt into my conscious mind. I was seeking reassurance—hoping, yet not knowing what I was hoping for.

Then, in the deafening silence, I heard a still, small voice, one I had heard before but which now seemed strangely unfamiliar. It was His voice, made unfamiliar because of my doubt and because of my fear. In spite of those doubts and fears, in spite of my questions, there was no mistaking His utterance. He simply told me that I would write a book, a book about my life and experiences of my journey as a Christian.

This was a strange sort of irony. You see, years before, when I was newly baptized, I had asked God in a lamenting tone why He had given me all these talents. I had spent decades in the real estate business with moderate success, and I had written two novels which had garnered some acclaim. I had always held out the possibility of wealth and fame if I continued in the vein of investment real estate and writing Afrocentric mystery novels.

My writing skills benefited my real estate investing business, so it seemed a cruel circumstance to me to let my skills and dreams waste away.

However, I knew that how I ran my real estate business was "dog-eat-dog," and not Christlike. And I knew that those books were written when I was in a very different mindset and serving the enemy of souls. They were not complimentary to my Lord and Savior, so much so that I had gotten rid of them and disavowed them. Still, for a walk of faith and surrender, it felt like I was turning my back on a way of life I had known and was comfortable with. Yes, I guess I was murmuring, much like the children of Israel had murmured when they left Egypt.

On that overlook, on that misty morning, God showed me the plans He had for me, plans for good and not for evil. I would write a book to bring Him glory. I sat there, quietly and with uncertainty, but with a mustard seed of faith. Was this the answer that I had been hoping for? I wasn't sure. Then my phone rang and broke the silence into a thousand shards of glass. It was a woman from my church's prayer line, Breda Hines, who had remembered something I said. She called for the sole purpose of letting me know that I should write a book! She had been impressed by some of the experiences I had shared on the prayer line, and she called to tell me that. I sat there in amazement as God watered my mustard seed.

While I was still on the phone with Breda, I got another call. It was my oldest daughter, Alexandra. "What is wrong?" I thought to myself. She rarely, if ever, called me early in the morning. I told Breda I had to take the call, and she understood, while reiterating her suggestion that I write a book.

"What is it, Lexie?" I asked.

Her exact words escape me, but the conversation went something like this: "Dad, I was just thinking about the other night when we were talking about Nipsey Hussle and Sebi. You have a wealth of experience. You really should write a book!"

Shocked by her statement, it took me a moment to respond. "What do you mean?" I countered.

"I was just thinking about some of the things you were telling us at family worship. You should really give some thought to writing another book."

God does not waste time. My mustard seed had been watered twice. What more confirmation did I need? The testimony of two witnesses can indeed convict. However, now I had three. I had confirmation beyond a shadow of a doubt, but what would the book be about? How would I write it? What would be its title? All those questions would be answered in God's timing. I would have to wait on the title and my message. Waiting, I'd learn, is sometimes the most difficult thing to do, but also the most necessary.

A Call to Battle

The Christian life of sanctification is difficult in the sense that it is a constant and continuing process. As civilians who often forget that we are in a war, we aren't prepared, on our own, to fight the battle over our souls. Yet, we are in a war—the war of our lives. It is internal and external, mental and physical.

Ephesians 6 speaks about "wrestling." Wrestling involves physical contact, intimate contact, hand-to-hand combat, skin against skin. You taste your opponent's clammy sweat, feel his hot breath, and smell the odor of his skin. You see the malice in his eyes, and you know, because of this intimacy, that if he could devour you, he would. He has not one morsel of pity. He is relentless and there is no trick, lie, or deception that he won't use to cause you pain and to cut your life short. He delights in mental torture and anguish. He is the master of torment and diversion. That is the devil, the principality and power whom we wrestle against. Fortunately, we don't wrestle alone. We have an Intercessor, at whose very name the enemy trembles. He is the absolute ruler of all principalities and powers, in heaven and on earth. We call Him Jesus, and He has given us a promise:

> Jesus came up and said to them, "All authority (all power of absolute rule) in heaven and on earth has been given to Me."
>
> —*Matthew 28:18 AB)*

The Apostle Paul emphasized Christ's victory by saying:

> When He had disarmed the rulers and authorities [those supernatural forces of evil operating against us], He made a public example of them [exhibiting them as captives in His triumphal procession], having triumphed over them through the cross.
>
> —*Colossians 2:15 AB*

Clearly, our victory has been won. The process of sanctification is growing to know the Victor, to love the Victor, to live in His victory, and to externalize His victory by sharing it with others. That is what this book describes, how God has worked in me to do those things.

My Story, His Glory

I have decided to tell *My Story, His Glory* in three parts of a series. The series is called, "Understanding the Angels of Revelation." By doing this, I believe it will expose *My Story, His Glory* to a wider reading audience. Larger books can be intimidating, and many people just don't have the time or the desire to read long narratives. Smaller books are also more likely to be shared from friend to friend and recommended to others. Finally, new concepts can be evaluated and assimilated better if they are introduced separately and in bite-sized chunks. To many of you who read these books, I will be sharing new spiritual, historical, and scientific concepts that go counter to what you have previously learned.

In the first installment, I will cover aspects of my life and experiences that I expect many of you will consider "common ground" and can relate to. Some of you will know what it is like to come from a dysfunctional home. You have experienced racism firsthand and felt the sting of the untimely death of a loved one. You have asked hard questions about life and have been dissatisfied with the answers you were given. You may have blamed God for your failures, disappointments, and griefs and dismissed Him from your life because of them. This is the common ground so many of us have traveled.

The second installment of *My Story, His Glory* will cover "uncommon ground." Uncommon ground relates to the application of biblical truths in our individual lives. *The word of God is alive and powerful.* In book two I will explain what alive and powerful means in practical terms. Every life event, every thought, and every action has eternal ramifications. I will share how this understanding transformed my life and my relationship with God. My understanding of God's plan for my life, my call, and His plans for all humanity—that includes you—is part of this study. Book two will explain where we are in this world's history and how we got here. We will study God's final warning and his soon to be fulfilled promise— Christ's second coming! Uncommon ground reveals the Bible in history and prophecy, their inseparability. The news tells you what happened— our exploration of the Bible will tell you why it happened and what will happen next. You will see yourself in our study—you are part of God's autobiography, the Holy Bible! You are part of the life of God, connected as a child is to their parents, as a husband to his wife. Uncommon ground exposes you to that truth in a way that will change you forever, for better or worse.

The third and final installment of *My Story, His Glory* is where we discuss "higher ground." Higher ground is the synthesis of truth. It is the dispelling of deception, lies, and falsehoods. The innuendoes of deceit embedded in our consciousness and secreted in our DNA are exposed and disarmed. God's word and His will are manifested purely, the whole truth and nothing but the truth. Rather, we believe and live or choose to be disobedient and die. The choice will be clearly ours individually. Like Christ at Gethsemane, our choice will be borne of anguish and in finality. Higher ground provides a revelation of our collective future and a warning. It is a revelation I experienced firsthand, and it is a warning I am compelled to share. Most of all, it is a hope and a promise given to each one of us. God bless you and our journey together.

CHAPTER I

The Wind Blows Where It Will

✝ *The wind blows wherever it wants. Just as you can hear the wind but can't tell where it comes from or where it is going, so you can't explain how people are born of the Spirit.*

—JOHN 3:8 NLT

The summers of 1972 and 1973 were seminal for me, a life at the "crossroads." I was on the cusp of manhood. I would be finishing high school, and like many adolescents, I was searching. I was conscripted to an uncertain future and a precarious hope. I had no real career plans. Behind me were bicycles, comic books, and hanging out in Georgetown. Ahead of me were SAT exams, prom outfits, and career choices. My last year of complete adolescent bliss was 1973. I needed to spend it wisely.

The popular movies and music of those summers provided the usual distractions. Hot Chocolate's song, "Brother Louie," a song about a teenage interracial couple, was a popular theme song reflecting the tenor of the times. I also liked the soft, sensual vocals of Roberta Flack's "Killing Me Softly." Those were sedating and distracting influences in a world that had too many questions and not enough answers.

My closest friends lived within a two-block radius of my house. Some of us had been together since elementary school, and some had moved to the Hillcrest neighborhood of D.C., better known to us locals as "soufheast." There was Eddie, who lived right next door. He was considered a pretty boy by some of the neighborhood girls. He was of mixed German American descent. He also played on the basketball team as a guard. His sister, Carmen, was also in our class. Being his neighbor and friend brought me some minor prestige.

There was Stewart, a shy giant, who as center on that same basketball team would lead our junior high school, Sousa, to win the citywide basketball championship that year. He was later recruited by Coach John Thompson, who was at St. Anthony's High School at that time. Yes, the girls loved Stewart too. My fortune was doubled.

Christopher was a year behind me in school, and like me, he had a passion for comics. We bonded immediately. His sister, Lisa, was a year behind him in school, and they lived within eyesight of my house.

Andre lived two blocks east and was given a variety of nicknames by Stewart. One was, "Mad Mannix," which was taken from a popular television detective show at that time. The name stuck with Andre for a good while. It described him to the "t." He would hit, or in that day's vernacular, "steal," you in the chest without notice or provocation. At least that was the case with some of us, but Andre had a good heart. Artie lived on the next block and was in the same class as Chris. He was the good guy of the bunch, but his older brother, Lonnie, was another story.

Lonnie would become a founding member of the "funk mob." It is hard for me to describe the funk mob but to simply say they were cool, loud, audacious, and they were pure "soufheast" D.C. Some of the things the funk mob did were wild, even for our era and neighborhood. It was one of those things where you had to be there to understand! There were others too, Lonnie's age and up.

My cousin, Morris, who stayed with us, had a best friend, David, who lived across from Stewart, one block down. They and others were in our neighborhood circle but not really part of our "inner" circle, since they were two to three years older. My younger brothers, Ullysee and Willie Clarence, were part of the household but much too young to be part of our circle. I had other cousins that were part of these formative years: Marcheta, Pamela, Terry, and Donna, also known as Nu Nu. I have heart-warming stories about each of them. Of course, there were many girls in our neighborhood too, but they pretty much congregated among themselves. There was the occasional boyfriend-girlfriend pairing, but it wasn't too serious—at least not quite yet.

To complete my circle of male friends was Daniel, the newest transplant to the neighborhood. He also had a sister, Pamala. He had gone to a mostly White middle school, Woodward Preparatory. As I recall, he arrived in Hillcrest his first year of high school, which at that time was the tenth grade. He lived directly behind Chris.

We had all been thrown together by happenstance in a disjointed world that was as disparate as our backgrounds. I can look back on our individual foibles and see real dysfunction in us and in our families, but let me start with my own.

Too Too "O" Foe!

2204 32nd Place SE was my actual home address so my brothers and I dallied with the idea of writing a book about our experiences growing up there. Our tentative title was *Too Too "O" Foe*, our modern negro spiritual, an ode born of the shared affliction we called childhood. We decided against writing it because we agreed that people reading it wouldn't believe that our story was true. It's amazing how much dysfunction people can become comfortable with. In an insane world insanity is the norm and that held true for us.

I lived with my mother, Gwendolyn, my step-father Ullysee Sr., and my cousin, Lydell, nicknamed Bubba. Bubba and mom were born only three days apart and grew up together in Mobile. Their relationship grew complicated over the years and eventually ended in animosity upon Bubba's death. My two younger brothers Ullysee and Willie completed the nucleus of the family along with Morris Arnold. Morris, nicknamed Blue, had been adopted by Nettie, my grandmother, and bequeathed to my mother after she died. My cousin Terry had lived with us for several years prior to our move, but went home to Mobile at the beginning of the school year. Morris stayed and we considered him our "cousin," although no formal adoption papers had ever been signed. His was a complicated story as well. We also had three dogs, Trixie, Duke, and Tiki, and a slew of unnamed critters. We had birds, fish, and rabbits during our stay in soufheast. This menagerie completed our blended family.

We lived in the nation's capital—the big city—and because of that, there was always a carousel of relatives and friends that came to visit and stay in hope of new opportunity. Let me add to that list of guests' babysitters who came to watch over my brothers while my mom worked. I believe we were comfortable with this constant traffic flow of family because it was what we grew up with in Mobile. I had always regarded it as our southern legacy. In Mobile, all my family lived within four blocks of one another, except for my uncle James, who died at 32 and lived with his wife and two daughters. Such close proximity bred familiarity and the tensions that came with its related contempt. For good or bad, family was family, and whether we got along well or not, we were blood and that meant helping each other out. So, when we moved north for better opportunity, some family came along.

That three bedroom, two-and-a-half-bathroom house was a home to many of my Alabama family. At first Terry, Morris, and I stayed in a single bedroom upstairs, but as family migrated in and out, that arrangement changed. We had the basement redone, including the garage, to accommodate the traffic. Cycling in and out were my cousins Deborah, Ben, Arthur, Sylvia, and her husband Carl. My uncle Nathaniel helped with some of the renovations and ended up staying for an extended period of time. His daughter Pamela spent her high school years with us. Vivian, also a first cousin, spent time with us as she took care of Ullysee while mom worked.

We had other babysitters which we imported from Mobile and Texas. Ruby was one of them until she got pregnant and had to return home to Alabama. That scandal caused a fracture in the family for a good while as relatives took sides on who was responsible. There were others, none of them blood relations—I can remember their faces but not their names. We even took in our next-door neighbors, the Davis's, for a short time when they sold their house and didn't have a place to go. They were a family of seven! Even though that situation was difficult and came with drama, we made the best of it.

Growing up I thought all of this was normal, a Southern way of life that was typical, where people cared for family and the community strays. It was normal for us. It was a normalcy of confusion resulting from the sins that so easily beset us. Much like the confusion in the world at large, it was all we knew. In my heart, though, I longed for peace.

If you can't imagine the tensions that arose from such living arrangements, that's a blessing. To experience it, was not. There were constant arguments, many resulting in physical altercations. There was verbal abuse and too much daily "messiness" to even dare try to chronicle. Our proximity exposed each of us to distinct and unshielded dysfunction as the world called it. An unfiltered description is just plain, old fashioned sin. In that parade of family and friends we had six alcoholics, one bisexual, three homosexuals, and one admitted murderer (although never brought to justice). Of course, there were the run of the mill sins that added to the daily mayhem. Even our pets weren't exempt, as a policeman nearly shot Duke for biting his boot. I think you can see why my brothers and I never wrote the book. The insanity of it was too painful and too surreal. Still there were somethings that even we found beyond the pale. What I share now is one of them.

Ullysee Sr. told us that his mother had died when he was young. That was a lie. Through other relatives, my mother found out that his mother was very much alive but had been in a mental asylum for nearly 50 years. Immediately, and in line with our family character, my mother got her released and brought her to live with us. She was frail, wheelchair-bound, and indistinguishable from a White person as far as complexion. She had long, straight salt-and-pepper hair, and she barely spoke, but you could tell she enjoyed living with family. She had a bad habit that caused much consternation. She would spit in the house—on the floor, on curtains, wherever. We were never able to fully break her of that habit. Still, we made room for her in our home and in our hearts. She stayed with us until she died.

There was rarely a dull moment at too too "o" foe—if it wasn't one thing it was another; much of it started with alcohol. Some alcoholics drink in seclusion and stay to themselves. Ullysee Sr. was not one of those. His drinking binges took on a different edge. He had a favorite chair in the dining room by the window. On his off days, he would get his vodka bottle and glass and stare into space. After he'd gotten sufficiently drunk, his mouth would twist slightly and he would become belligerent. He was a loud drunk, and so was Bubba—fortunately they got drunk on different days of the week. Ullysee had a pistol and he would brandish it and threaten us with bodily harm, especially during a long binge. It was so bad that we had to barricade ourselves behind locked doors until he sobered up. Reflecting on those times, I shake my head and thank God for His grace.

Through all of it though, I give my mother credit. She held fast to her faith in a house full of apostates. We, all the boys, went off to church every Sunday, rain or shine. Pennsylvania Avenue Baptist Church was only five blocks away from our house. It was nearly all White like our neighborhood when we moved to southeast in 1967. I remember the choir singing in their matching robes. There was only one Black person, a woman, in the choir of maybe 30 people. I would watch her and wonder how she felt being surrounded by White people. I didn't envy her because our neighborhood was the same way at first, but that changed quickly.

The assassination of Martin Luther King Jr. and the riots that followed his death accelerated White flight from a trickle to a flood. I was nearly 12-years-old, but it seemed I'd lived a full three-score and 10 already. I felt old in my bones and weary from a struggle that was only starting. But, as I think about the trauma of those years, I can't help but praise God for His love, compassion, and faithfulness. His hand was always present, unravelling every knot of adverse circumstance, mending every broken loss, and salvaging every ruined life. Just like with Jacob's family in the Bible, his 12 sons by four women, was wrought with dysfunction and strife, so was ours. But just like God had done with Jacob and his family, God would do with us. God made right what we couldn't. My family and Jacob's are a microcosm of the world. God will make right what we can't.

I've just described the nuclear forces that molded me up to that point. My new environment with my new friends would add another layer to the combustion of strife. The strife in my family and in the world around me had made me who I was and formulated my beliefs on who I could become. I was about to enter into a new phase of life. I was not prepared.

Ready or Not, Here I Come

The social and cultural forces of 1960s America had molded our desires, expectations, and beliefs, especially mine and those of my friends. Yet, in our naivete, we thought that our beliefs were our own—uniquely who we were—self-formed and managed, not grafted into us by influences and forces that we barely knew existed and could not give a name to. On the small screen, with anguished detail, we had witnessed the assassinations of Martin, Malcolm, and the Kennedys. We weathered the riots and watched America set aflame by frustrated men that looked like us, though slightly older.

We had seen the flag-draped coffins of Vietnam veterans, until we were full of hate for a system that denied our usefulness unless it was as target practice for domestic police or to subdue foreign victims of American aggression. We had endured the bitterness of a second civil war, which was politely called the civil rights movement, knowing that the American power structure would never fulfill its promise of "forty acres and a mule," at least not to us. Segregation and forced busing, housing discrimination and White flight, Black Power protests, and White backlash were the star-spangled canopy that hung over us all. It fomented a spirit of apathy, distrust, and outright rebellion.

Having witnessed the murder of our political leaders, we took time to reassess. Our new heroes were Ali, Brown, and Abdul-Jabbar—men who dominated their respective sports and walked with a swag or "pimp," which we all practiced to imitate. They were a clear threat to the White American psyche, but less likely to be taken out with a bullet. These too were men who looked like us but were slightly older. Society didn't really care for them, but it had to respect them, nonetheless. That is how society felt about us, too. To mainstream American culture, we were young and Black, which made us armed and dangerous. They preferred to build prisons to contain us, rather than schools to educate us.

At 16, going on 17, that was my world; a confusing contradiction which was maddening. It was the hardening cement that would hold my feet in place until I would cease to resist the dissonance. Its goal was to kill me off quickly or place me in a brick-and-mortar 8'x 8' cell. It would steal my health, cripple my dreams, and then blame me for my own failures.

That is who I was—I inhabited a world of clear distinctions. As young, Black men, that is who we were. And into this world, my world, stepped the graying matriarch of my family, Annie Mae Sellers. She had come from Mobile, Alabama to visit her youngest sister, my mother, Gwendolyn Wood. She had known firsthand what segregation was and what the authentic America was, behind the white lie of equality. She knew it far better than I did, but she still had a hope that I was not familiar with.

CHAPTER 2

A New Perspective
on an Old Belief

✝ *Behold, I will do a new thing; now it shall spring forth; shall*
ye not know it? I will even make a way in the wilderness, and
rivers in the desert.

—ISAIAH 43:19 KJV

A*nnie Mae was a strong woman, short* and stout. She had light skin—her birth certificate designated her as a "mulatto," but there was nothing mixed about her personality. She wore her hair long, in Native American-like braids, one on each side of her head.

In our family, we have legends about Annie Mae that are repeated to this day. She had a strange religion, too. She called herself a Seventh-day Adventist. Family legend says that, while she attended a tent meeting in 1947, against the wishes of her family, she accepted the advent message.

Her Uncle Claude, my great uncle, threatened to cut her neck from ear to ear if she did not recant. I once witnessed him using a pocketknife to stab a woman he had been dating. We all looked on in horror as the blood squirted from the wound in her head with each heartbeat. This was in front of our house, so he was probably crazy enough to attempt to do Annie Mae harm. Annie Mae never recanted, and he never touched her. Her son, Charlie, would later attribute her protection to the Holy Spirit.

To be sure, there were others in my family that took their stand and left their Southern Baptist traditions for this strange faith. My mother and her brother James nearly did but were turned away by White men who thought themselves ready for heaven but were evidently not ready for church desegregation. This was truly a contradiction of values but, after all, this was Mobile, Alabama, where the last ship carrying kidnapped Africans had unloaded its human contraband on American shores. The Clotilda was its name, and the year was 1860 when it was illegally secreted into Mobile Bay.

Annie Mae was no-nonsense, and when she talked to me, she naturally had my full attention. On one particular Saturday, which is the Seventh-day Sabbath of Genesis, while she was visiting with us, she took me to church with her. The steepled edifice, DuPont Park Seventh-day Adventist Church, was near our house. It was like "regular" church, but just on Saturday. It was larger than the Baptist church that I attended at that time, and I felt comfortable there. There were many young people my age in the congregation too, but they seemed different. I couldn't quite figure out how; but I felt it, nonetheless.

Shortly after leaving church, Annie Mae asked me, "Petey (that was my nickname), what do you think of our church?" I wasn't quite sure what she meant, but I answered anyway. "It was good, just different though."

"Different, in what way?"

"Well, it's Saturday! That's real different!"

"Yes, that's true, it is Saturday and it's what the Bible calls the Lord's day. The Lord's day is called the Sabbath. Do you know why I go to church on the sabbath?"

"Yes, it's in the Ten Commandments."

"That's right," she replied. I felt proud of myself for my answer. She continued.

"Keeping the Sabbath holy is especially important right now." I responded with a forceful, "Why?"

"Because Jesus is coming back soon. In fact so soon that we both might see Him come in the clouds! A lot of people don't like to talk about that and a lot of other people think you're crazy if you believe it. Do you believe it, that Jesus is coming soon?" I thought for a moment before I answered.

"Yeah, I think so. Why do you think so?" I could see by her expression that she was glad I asked.

"You see all the things going on in the world, you see all the people getting killed, the accidents and wars? Look at the people in our own family that have died. Those things weren't supposed to happen but God's enemy made it all happen."

"You mean the devil?"

"Yes, that's right. The devil, Satan, is the cause of all the world's pain, suffering, and death. But when Jesus comes back, He's going to destroy the devil! And He's going to set up a new kingdom where none of those things will exist. Think about it. There will be no more pain or dying. People will live forever in perfect health. You will live forever, Petey."

I was a comic book connoisseur with the biggest collection of all my peers, probably at least two thousand at that time, both DC and Marvel. So, what she said was right down my alley. Clearly, I was no stranger to fantasy, but Annie Mae was nothing but the truth. What she said had to be fact, not fiction. I took it as such.

With unrestrained excitement, I asked her, "Will I be able to fly?"

"When 'the great controversy' is over we all will be able to fly. We'll all be able to go to any planet in the sky and meet the people that live there. You can visit them whenever you want, forever and ever. Isn't that amazing, Petey."

"Yes!" I quickly retorted. She continued.

"But before that time comes, many terrible things will happen. The Bible calls it the time of Jacob's Trouble and it will be even worse than now."

Annie Mae provided compelling details as she spoke. "As the end approaches, the world will be in a great state of turmoil, like nothing it has ever seen. There will be wars and climate calamities. There will be signs in the heavens, great and strange things happening upon the earth. People will be afraid, looking for answers and looking for some way out."

Everything she said could have come straight out of the pages of The Fantastic Four or Thor. She continued, "And the whole world will turn against God's people."

I asked, "What about America?"

"Yes, America too—especially America. America is a beast!"

Her words were visceral and they startled me. America a beast? That was contrary to what I had been educated to believe. America was the land of the free and the home of the brave. How could that be? Was she talking about the racism with its companion violence and terrorism that we'd both survived? What did she mean? The contradiction was piercing as was my response. I asked. "Really!"

She continued.

"Yes, really. America is actually the beast that comes out of the earth with two horns. She has the horns of a lamb but speaks like a dragon. She appears one way, like a lamb, but acts another way, like a dragon. America, will lead the whole world to come against God's people."

"Wow," I said in amazement. She continued, "It will be nighttime, and even in that darkness, God's people will be surrounded by an even darker gloom. Every government in the world will issue a decree against us, as the Bible says, to kill those who 'Keep the commandments of God and have the faith of Jesus'. Remember the Sabbath; that's the main commandment that will be at the center of the great controversy (see Revelation 12:17). They will establish a time when it will be lawful to kill anyone who keeps the Sabbath commandment."

Until then, I'd looked at the Sabbath as just another day. At that moment, I understood it wasn't. It was special to God and that meant it should be special to me. She continued.

"As the hour to kill God's people approaches, people all over the world will move with their guns in hand to kill God's people with one decisive blow. Then right before they can kill them, they see the night sky light up and a beautiful rainbow appears. It spans the sky from east to west and seems to cover each huddled company of God's faithful people. The attackers stop dead in their tracks. Raised weapons are dropped to their sides and their mocking cries cease. Their anger and hate are replaced by a crippling terror at the spectacular sight and for what they fear the rainbow means."

I questioned her. "A rainbow at night, Aunt Annie Mae?"

"Yes, the Bible says that the rainbow is the sign of God's covenant, His promise. Then, there is heard a loud voice that shakes the very air. It's unlike any voice heard before. It is clear and majestic and unmistakable. The words ring out from everywhere and all at once. *Look up!*"

In my suspense, I barely uttered, "Wow!" She looked at me with a piercing gaze.

"God's people, who had been cringing in terror only moments before in fear of their lives, now stand erect with hands reaching toward the sky.

The sky parts and in the middle is the Son of God. Christ is seated upon His throne, high and lifted up. Surrounding Him are millions of angels. The sky is lit with His glory. The words of victory ascend to the throne of the Savior. All creation is in an uproar— signs and wonders appear in the sky. The wicked cry for the rocks to fall on them; the righteous proclaim, "Lo, this is our God; we have waited for Him, and he will save us" (Isaiah 25:9 KJV). Then there is a mighty earthquake such as never has been on the earth. Then the trump of God sounds and all the righteous dead come up from their graves and they, with the righteous living, walk on air to meet Jesus."

I was breathless at Annie Mae's words, but I wanted to know more. I queried, "Is all this stuff in a book?"

"Yes, it's in the Bible and a book called The Great Controversy. I'll make sure you get them."

"Wow, thanks, Aunt Annie Mae!"

Annie Mae shared the story with a confidence that was contagious. It was clear she believed every word she spoke. She ended with the opinion that she would see all those things happen in her lifetime. I wondered if that was possible. I hoped it was. Jesus' parable of the Sower who sows seed is relevant here. Annie Mae had sown a seed in fertile, adolescent soil. I was fascinated by the hope and the possibilities. The meaning that I was searching for and could not define began to take form. It would take time, but the seed would grow.

My Last Year at Anacostia High School

Annie Mae's words colored the remaining days of my summer with hope. I had a new purpose and I wasn't as doubtful of my future. In August, preparations for my final year started in earnest. New clothes and school supplies had to be bought and farewells made to neighbors moving away and friends going off to college. That was part of the summer ritual and the parties that came along with it. As often happens in life, the emotions of melancholy and excitement mixed into a reflective cocktail on the future. When the summer ended, I found myself a senior at Anacostia High School, one of the poorest and roughest schools in the District of Columbia. I was told the average grade at the school was a "D," and until that year, I had been an average student. Now, I needed to buckle down. If I were going to go to college, I had to get better grades. I had never been a "dumb" student, but in the group I hung with, smart was square. I had to change my attitude.

Fortunately, that year I was blessed with teachers who inspired and motivated me. Mrs. Jefferson, an English teacher with a civil rights pedigree, was a force to be reckoned with. She was prim and proper with perfect diction—a textbook teacher. Mr. Ratner, a Jewish man and our art teacher, had a love for his students and gained their respect for it. Mr. Levy was also Jewish and the civil government teacher. There was Colonel Brewington, who had retired as an Army colonel and was a no-nonsense instructor reminiscent of a drill sergeant. Mrs. Pratt was the assistant principal, and I understood that she was a close relative of Sharon Pratt Dixon, who would become the mayor of our fair city. Mrs. Pratt and I were on a first-name basis. I had been in her office on several occasions, none of them for good cause.

Once, during the third quarter of my senior year, I was late for class, and Mrs. Pratt caught me in the hall. Over my very vocal protest, she commanded me to come to her office. I had given her the real reason why I was late for class. I'd just been talking and not paying attention to the time. I assured her that I was a changed man, no longer cutting class or playing chess for money. It was of no effect. She sat me down in her office and pulled out my folder. She looked it over, and then looked at me. She started, "Mr. Arnold, I am looking over your grades." I tried to interrupt her.

"Quiet, Mr. Arnold!" She looked at me and started again. "I see here that you have mostly As and Bs, and in the hardest classes and with the best teachers we have!"

I didn't know what to say. Was she implying that I was cheating?

She continued, "Mr. Arnold, I am disappointed in you. If you had applied yourself your first two years here, you could have been one of our best students. You could have gotten scholarships to whatever school you wanted. I would have seen to it." I knew she would have too. She paused, and I was still speechless. I looked away, chagrined by her remarks.

She finished. "Mr. Arnold, you will do well. I am proud of you." Suddenly, I felt encouraged. As I left her office, hope sprang in my heart. I could go to college, and I could make it in spite of what America felt about boys like me. Mrs. Pratt was a hard woman to please, but she was truthful and fair. I was confident I would meet others like her in my future journey.

The final teacher of note for me was Dr. Jacob Justiss, who taught African American history. I remember the first day in his class. He told us to pick up our history books and turn to the first chapter and page. We did. He then proceeded to read from the text. After he finished reading, he looked up at the class and said, "Everything I just read is a lie!" Then he threw the book in the trashcan. We were stunned by Dr. Justiss' abrupt action, but applauded his audacity. I don't remember the book or what he read but his act will always be a part of our shared legacy.

Instantly, I knew I was in the right place. I felt a magnetic affinity for him. He also happened to be a retired Seventh-day Adventist pastor. He had pastored the church, DuPont Park, that Annie Mae had taken me to on that Sabbath. He pastored there in the early sixties. That could not have been a coincidence. I was drawn to him because of his love for who he was, a self-assured Black man, and because of the Adventist beliefs that he wove into American history. He watered the seed that my aunt had planted. The odd beliefs that she told in story form, he expounded to me in detail. The sanctuary service, Sabbath worship, vegetarianism, and end-times prophecies of Daniel and Revelation would lead me down a new and different path. It also fit well into the collage of beliefs that I shared with my circle of neighborhood friends.

Hillcrest Ecumenism

My friends and I were an eclectic bunch when it came to our religious beliefs. Eddie was an Episcopalian, but he would become a practicing Buddhist and spent time at an ashram in the Midwest. Stewart, born into the Southern Baptist tradition, would become a Black Muslim with Masonic influences and frequented Saviors' Day events in Chicago. Chris was also Baptist. He moved to Columbia, South Carolina at the end of his ninth-grade school year and switched to the Church of God in Christ. Artie and Lonnie were Seventh-day Adventists, but I didn't know that at the time.

I never knew what Andre believed, since he never spoke about religion. I remember trying to give him a tract once, but he would have none of it.

Daniel had a unique mix of ideologies. His dad, Palmer Botts, was a poet and, as I recall, taught yoga. Mr. Botts was also very vocal about the plight of Black men in America. He was sincere, and I liked him a lot. Daniel was very much like his dad. In fact, after we graduated from high school, he spent the summer in India learning the art of meditation and the Hindu religion. Both he and Stewart changed their names. Stewart became Rashid, and Daniel became Daoud.

This religious menagerie seemed normal, a Hillcrest ecumenism of sorts, and was encouraged in our small circle. Our form of ecumenism meant no one was wrong and subsequently that no one was right. This satanic delusion, brotherly togetherness superior to love and obedience to God was our stew of beliefs and was never questioned. That same delusion has infected the world today. The underlying flavor that bound it and us together was our distrust and dislike of a racist America. We were all searching for an understanding and explanation of the meaning of it all. But I didn't have to search anymore. I found the books of Daniel and Revelation fascinating, as shared by Dr. Justiss. Their prophecies, coded in signs and symbols, were better than comic book storylines. They were real, and they applied to me and everyone I knew. The prophecies had eternal implications.

Even though I had gained a different perspective, I still attended the Baptist church and was living like most of the nominal Christians I knew. I had no real impetus to change—then it happened, the catalyst for change. Dan and I went to Georgetown to watch a movie that had been partly filmed there. It was called *The Exorcist*, and had been released to theaters the day after Christmas 1973. When we saw it in the second week of January, the theater on Wisconsin Avenue was so crowded that we couldn't get in. So, we waited in the parking lot, resting on the hood of a stranger's car, stargazing. We smoked a couple of joints while trying to keep warm. We waited there until the next show time. By the time we got into the movie theater, we were so high that we laughed throughout the entire show.

Then we sat through it again, but by that time our high had worn off. The movie scared me nearly to death. I still recall the opening scene with the dogs fighting in the desert and the eerie feeling that it gave me. Of course, the scenes of the young girl's possession and her head turning backward made me shiver. I knew demon possession was real—I'd read it in the Bible. I went home that night realizing the power of the enemy and feeling my estrangement from God. If God wasn't on my side, then I was at the devil's mercy. But the thing is, the devil has no mercy! I slept with two or three Bibles that night, if I slept at all. I began to pray for mercy and began to go to "sabbath" church on a regular basis.

Things began to happen that strengthened my resolve. In April the police called on a cold and rainy Sunday morning to tell us that Morris, who had left home less than a year before, had been arrested and taken to St. Elizabeth's Hospital. They found him naked on the National Mall firing a gun and screaming that God is a fish. Later, before graduation, the Gideon Bible people, a charity whose primary mission was to give Bibles to all classes, came to Anacostia and passed out Bibles to many of the students. It was like a mini revival at our school. Suddenly, it was okay to believe in the Bible without being ridiculed. People I knew but had never considered religious were carrying Bibles. I remember seeing one guy in the hall—all I knew about him was that he was loud and unruly in class, but he was reading his Bible right out in the open! It could have been for show, but who was I to judge? I took it all as a sign that what Annie Mae and Jacob Justiss told me was true—Jesus was coming again. Too many things were happening for it to be a coincidence. I needed to be ready!

My cousin, Arthur Sellers, attended the same church that Jacob Justiss did in Southwest D.C., Brotherhood Seventh-day Adventist, and I started attending with him. It was an exciting time for me. I started "feeling" church and taking Bible classes. I began to commit my time and energy to God. I could see how good God had been to me. I had taken His favor for granted. Feeling church was embracing God, really. As I studied more independently, I was convicted to share what I knew with others in my neighborhood. I literally went door to door sharing what I had learned. Of course, my "boys", Stewart in particular, came up with a nickname for me "The Rev." It stuck. It was funny to them, but it didn't matter to me. I was convicted, and before long, I was baptized into the Seventh-day Adventist church. This was just in time for me to go to college.

A Strange New World

That same spring, I was baptized at Brotherhood Church. Stewart was my only neighborhood friend in attendance. After church they had a potluck dinner prepared with vegetarian food that was quite tasty. Stewart and I were both impressed with the meal and the people. I still have a picture of that event. High school graduation soon followed and then it was done. I had turned a corner in my life. I was about to enter a strange new world. I prayed about college and what would be my area of study. Theology seemed to be what God had called me to do, but like Jimmy Cliff's song, I had "many rivers to cross" to make that a reality.

The summer of 1974 was packed with maneuverings to get me into college. I didn't have the money and I didn't have a clue of what to do, but my family rallied to help me. There was a Seventh-day Adventist college in Takoma Park, so I applied there and was accepted. I had done well on the SAT, and even though my grades had improved, Columbia Union College still placed me on academic probation for my first semester. Suddenly, I was thrust into a predominately White world, and a religious one at that. In so many ways, I was not prepared for the transition. What made it even harder was the fact that I still lived at home. I had one foot in my old world and one foot in the new one. Even now as I recall it, it seemed surreal to me. Everything was new—faces, places, and dreams.

At first, I didn't have a car or a driver's license. Fortunately, some of the young people from DuPont Church who lived near me in Southeast, James Vines, Denise Malone, and Cassandra Danley, commuted to Takoma Academy high school, right down the street from my college. At the time, little did I suspect that Cassandra would one day become my wife. I remember them being so animated all the time, or maybe I was just shy. They had all grown up together, and I was truly an outsider. I had no Adventist pedigree and I was shy by nature. I tried to blend into my new environment. I'm not sure if I succeeded, but I remember those times as being good.

My years in college had a positive influence on me. I made many new friends and gained a very different perspective on life, God, and religion. I became a vegetarian, at least for a time, and was more health conscious. I caught a glimpse of the hope I'd seen in Aunt Annie Mae a few years earlier. There was an underlying belief that life had a meaning and purpose. That was part of the Adventist culture. I loved many things about the Adventist lifestyle, but there was one thing that seemed steadfastly the same—racism.

The cordial apartheid prevailing in America at that time was well ensconced on our campus too. Adventism, once the beacon of American racial liberalism, had long before surrendered the moral high ground to conservative evangelical bigoted mores. On campus, by and large the different ethnic groups congregated among themselves. There were only two mixed romantic relationships among students: one was in the open, the other in secret and the tension they both caused was real. The seating in the cafeteria and for student worships also followed ethnic lines. Of course, these were not codified regulations, but they were adhered to nonetheless. When they were broken, there was obvious discomfort. I'll share three personal stories to bring home the validity of my perspective. The first was when I moved on campus.

There was real and visible segregation on our campus, but I believe Columbia Union College made a valiant effort to begin reconciliation of the races in my freshman year as a student there. I'm not sure about the back-room machinations, how it came about, but I was one of four Black students to have a White roommate. His name was Timothy Dolan and he was a freshman theology major like myself. We had to both agree to this living arrangement and it was an experiment with an uncertain outcome. I was from the inner-city and, as I recall, Tim was from a small town in Ohio. Would our integration be combustible and explode in flames, or would it be the first step in a new order of brotherhood? It was neither of those extremes. We became more than cordial but less than friends. Our lukewarm relationship reflected our church at large when it came to racial issues. Still, the experiment was worth the effort even though we have long since lost touch. I remember Tim fondly.

This second story is revealing about campus attitudes and speaks for itself. Bob M. shared a dorm room not far from mine at Morrison Hall. He hadn't been an Adventist for long and his conversion came after a bad car accident that nearly took his life. He lost an eye in the accident and still had the scars and limp to remind him of God's favor. He was Puerto Rican but had moved to New Jersey. He was jovial with a grand smile—we became good friends. We went on double dates together and hung out quite a bit. As I recall, he majored in health science so we didn't have any classes together, as my major was theology. We were all busy with classes, but after a while I began to spend less and less time with Bob. Even in the dorm hall he seemed to be less talkative and sometimes even distant. It bothered me and I wondered what I had done. I wondered what was wrong. It bothered Bob too. Finally, he told me what had happened. We talked after Sabbath dining hall. I started.

"We're going bowling tonight and then will grab a Ledo's pizza. You want to hang with us?"

He thought for a minute, maybe pondering the good times we'd had doing that exact thing and considering why he'd stopped. His reply was candid and it was what I needed to hear.

"Nate, I'm sorry man, I can't go. You know I've got this scholarship." He hesitated. "The truth is, I could lose my scholarship. You know, I can't mention any names, but I was called into a meeting. They told me I was spending too much time with the wrong people. They told me I needed to associate with other people. I needed to make new friends."

He didn't need to tell me who the people who made the suggestion were or who the new friends should be—I had a strong suspicion. I was shocked about the fact that they were so blatant about it though. I pretended I wasn't hurt as I spoke with disdain in my voice.

"We are all supposed to be Christians. That's messed up. I'm glad you told me though. Now it all makes sense. Man, do what you got to do."

There wasn't much to say after that. I had a scholarship and, although it wasn't a full ride, it helped me out a lot. I understood his dilemma and I didn't blame him at all. I harbored that hurt against the powers that be and their racist attitudes.

As time passed, we mended fences, but things were different. That was an incident I couldn't excuse or ignore. I had to call it what it was: racism.

There was another incident which left a scar I still trace from time to time with my mind's finger. I was a junior taking New Testament Greek. Our class was a small class, maybe around nine students. I was one of two African Americans in the class, the other was a female. She was petite and quiet. The professor resembled Colonel Sanders of Kentucky Fried Chicken fame and we awarded him the nickname Colonel K, behind his back of course. He was a minister as was his father. His father had been a missionary in Africa. As "Colonel K." was teaching class, he recalled the good times when he was a young boy growing up in Africa. His gaze grew distant as he carried us back through memory to the time and place of his youth. His nostalgic reminiscing was hypnotic and he seemed to be in a trance himself as he repeated his favorite ditty from that time. He said, "Eeny, meeny, miny, moe, Catch a nigger by the toe. If he hollers, let him go, Eeny, meeny, miny, moe."

His fond recollection would have continued except for the forced throat clearings and startled glances of those in attendance. He abruptly woke from his trance and simply said, "Maybe I shouldn't have said that." That was as near an apology as we would get. We finished the class that day and tried to forget what had happened. None of the White students ever mentioned it, but it was all us two Black students could really talk about. The female student resigned the class a short time after that, but I stuck it out for the rest of the semester. After all, the word "nigger" had been part of my vocabulary since my childhood. I must admit, it did sting though and it was one of the many slights that caused me to transfer to Oakwood College the next academic year. What cemented my decision was the "B" I got in that same class. Most if not all of my test scores were in the high 80s and 90s. Another older White student who never passed a single exam was given a "C"—his name was Cash and I liked him. That did not diminish the injustice. What the professor did was wrong, but it was the White thing to do. Cash would minister in an underserved part of the country, West Virginia, where he was from. I understood the reasoning. Discrimination always has good reasons, but it's still discrimination.

Christian apartheid is an oxymoron, but it is the spine of mainstream American Christianity. Its hypocrisy heaps scorn upon the church itself and upon our Lord, while the devils who formulated it congratulate themselves on their coup de grâce. This cancer in the church has caused untold damage to both Blacks and Whites and it has metastasized to every organ of Christian America. Hospice and death are where the church is now, I fear.

My Sojourn in Mecca

For sure, my honeymoon was over with the Adventist religion and had matured into a marriage with its regular discovery of blemishes and foibles. Columbia Union College was predominately White and subsequently had its own challenges, but there was another school, Oakwood College, in Huntsville Alabama. The school was also Adventist but predominately Black. I decided to go there for my next semester—that was January of 1977. I drove down with a friend, Roosevelt Rayford. We had attended the same junior high school, John Phillip Sousa. Sousa was eventually placed on the National Register of Historic Places because of its tie to school desegregation. The case was better known as Brown vs. Board of Education and was decided in 1954. It seems that issues of race relations have followed me throughout my life, or maybe race relations is part of America's DNA and subsequently mine. The answer to that question was no longer a conundrum for me as I motored my way to the state of my birth with my memories and trauma in tow.

Oakwood College sat on 380 acres of beautiful farmland in northern Alabama and was founded in 1896. Ellen G. White had been instrumental in its founding and felt that the site had been chosen by God. As a Black college, Oakwood was rich in history. Richard Wright had given it an honorable mention in his book *Native Son*. Arna Bontemps, a noted member of the Harlem Renaissance, and other notables like Little Richard, a founding father of rock and roll, had been teachers or students there. Eddie Davis, my old neighborhood friend, had also been enrolled there for a short time. Indeed, Oakwood was a mecca for African American Seventh-day Adventists, churning out pastors, doctors, teachers, and other professionals. My hopes were great for the school I'd heard so much about.

There were many people there that I knew, like Artie my childhood friend from Hillcrest. Other friends I'd made at CUC were transferring there also. Those were good omens.

Unfortunately, I was not financially cleared when I arrived, and neither was Rayford. We both, along with a slew of other students, would spend nearly two weeks getting registered and into classes. They had a large open area in the men's dorm that they converted and brought in about 20 cots for us to sleep on. That was where we stayed. Even when our financial clearance was resolved, we still needed to sign up for classes and get dorm rooms. The matriculation process was very different from what I'd experienced at CUC. The delay was not an auspicious start to my time there—still, I was excited. My roommate was Johnathan Watkins, who had also transferred from CUC. He was a member of Brotherhood Church and was Donna Smith's cousin. We got along well.

Once I finally started classes, I settled into a routine. My classes were not difficult and I did well, but something was missing and I couldn't quite figure out what it was. Oakwood's culture was similar to CUC's in many and important ways. The music program was outstanding and was integral to the spiritual life on campus. You had the theology majors who were on the fast track to success. Many were looking for "a call" and they would marry wives with Adventist pedigree to facilitate their success. There were the education majors, predominately women, many of whom would teach in Adventist schools and marry Adventist ministers. And, there were the pre-med and biology majors. Many of them would become leaders in their churches and the Adventist middle-class back home.

The Seventh-day Adventist Church has the second largest school system and hospital system in the world. Only the Catholic Church has larger school and hospital systems among church institutions, yet the Adventist church has only 21 million members as opposed to the Catholic Church-es' 1.3 billion! In the same line of comparison, the Catholic Church is over 1,600 years old, while the Adventist Church was founded during the American Civil War in 1863. This comparison of Protestant and Catholic faiths has significant implications in our time regarding biblical prophecy and will be expounded upon later. Indeed, God has blessed the Protestant movement and the Adventist Church in particular. The proof is visible for the world to see. Oakwood College was a significant part of God's blessing and the church's success.

Although my time at Oakwood was short, it was very enlightening. My experience in a predominately African American Seventh-day Adventist environment was different from what I had known, but there were real struggles to overcome. They were different struggles, but struggles none-theless. Trying to fit in, and trying to figure out life was something we all had to do whether we were Black or White. The sin problem and the struggles it creates is not a respecter of persons. We are all faced with similar issues and have similar temptations to overcome. The complexion of our problems may be different, they are superficial, as is the color of our skin, but the root cause is the same. I wasn't ready to admit that then, but the truth has a way of sticking with you until you're ready to hear it. I learned there that Mecca is not heaven.

I learned there what Jesus shared with His disciples: No matter how ma-jestic the temples we construct on earth they remain on cursed ground. "There shall not be left here one stone upon another" (Matthew 24:2). The structures we build, rather institutions or societies, are never an end in themselves. They are only useful as God makes them so. They can nev-er substitute for the majesty of heaven, nor were they ever meant too. Christ instructed us that heaven is our home and that we should place our treasures there, for only there will they last. That lesson was not com-pletely lost on me, but while on earth, I was still trying to figure out who I was and what my true calling was. I decided to do that closer to home and family.

A Dream Deferred

In my senior year, I came back to CUC with a new attitude and a new major. I changed my major from theology to psychology. I was still searching for those all-elusive answers—what made me and the world the way we were? It wasn't purely a White thing or a Black thing. I was beginning to realize that but I was still confused. No, the reality is, I was blinded and unable to see the truth of the human condition although it was right in front of me. Let me spell it out in capital letters: S-I-N. Sin is the cause of all our ills—it starts there and it ends there. Satan is the originator of sin. He is also the father of subterfuge and obfuscation. Oftentimes we aid him in his lies by clinging to our own cherished idols. Race had been an easy target to shoot at and I needed something to blame for all the pain and ills I'd suffered. The devil made sure I wouldn't blame him. The stronghold he'd erected in my mind so carefully and over so many years would not be torn down easily.

And Jesus said, For judgment I am come into this world, that they which see not might see; and that they which see might be made blind. And some of the Pharisees which were with him heard these words, and said unto him, Are we blind also? Jesus said unto them, If ye were blind, ye should have no sin: but now ye say, We see; therefore your sin remaineth.

—*John 39-41 KJV*

Like the Pharisees, I blindly made my way along, certain I had 20/20 vision. So, for my senior practicum I did a study on the correlation between racism and religiosity. My background provided the predilection for my subject, but I was hoping against hope that God's last-day people would be different than the general society. Martin Luther King Jr. said that "at

11 o'clock Sunday morning...we stand in the most segregated hour in America."[1] For Christians, that was not supposed to be the case, it was especially not supposed to be the case for the purveyors of the last day message given to humanity. As Adventists, we prided ourselves on the light we'd been given, but that light was hidden under a bed, not so much by our words, but by our actions. Our practice contradicted our preaching. How was that possible?

My research topic was chosen to bring clarity around that point for me, but I was surprised about the interest that my topic garnered from others, too. Other universities contacted me and asked to be alerted to my findings. But I wasn't so sure about my own department head. He was an older, White guy and he was cordial enough, but we never seemed to gel. In spite of my perceptions, I would not be deterred. I was able to get the surveys done and began to interview students on campus.

I soon realized that, far from being more progressive, or having Christian attitudes around racial issues, it was just the opposite. I remember the keen sense of disappointment I felt as I spoke to my White schoolmates. Some of them did not seem to realize that their prejudices were based on lies, and their subsequent attitudes were hurtful to people like me.

One interview stands out in particular. It was with a nursing major that started out as a freshman with me. She was attractive with pale white skin, deep blue eyes and dark hair. I choose her because I never saw her mingling with any students of color even though, in a school the size of ours you couldn't help run into people, but I don't recall her ever speaking to me. I'm not sure whose idea it was but we met on the campus lawn where the school welcome sign was in broad daylight. There was a large brick flower bed there three feet tall with two tall flag poles. We sat there and talked briefly before starting the interview. I wanted her to feel comfortable as she completed the questionnaire. Some of the questions were pointed and others innocuous, but I assured her that all her responses would be confidential and anonymous. What struck me about our inter-action was the emotional distance I felt. We were in close proximity, but it was like I wasn't a "real" person to her. Her responses to the questions gave me a sense of the "otherness" in which she regarded me and people that look like me. Even as I write this now, I still feel the numbness of that moment.

After the interviews and the tallying of my results, my fears were realized, the blinders had been removed and my eyes were open. SDA White rac-ism and privilege stung me like a slap in the face. The realization that the Seventh-day Adventist Christians I was going to share heaven with were no different than mainstream culture was a bitter pill for me to swallow, but I had no choice. I still had a lot to learn about people and the differ-ence between what they say and what they live.

> And herein lies the tragedy of the age: not that men are poor, –all men know something of poverty; not that men are wicked, –who is good? not that men are ignorant, –what is Truth? Nay, but that men know so little of men.[2]
>
> —*W. E. B. DuBois*

This tragedy I had come to understand. I also realized that the "double consciousness" so eloquently spoken about by W. E. B Dubois was real, and it was even more tangible for me living in the predominate culture. The dual discovery hit me like a ton of bricks, and it changed me at the core. The hope that I had embraced as a Seventh-day Adventist Christian was a lie, so I concluded. What else had I believed that was a lie?

I headed down a slippery slope, equating God with His flawed people, and the Creator with His fallen creature. It is a trap that the enemy lays out with meticulous detail. I didn't know it then, but I had fallen victim to the same deception the enemy has used for eons. Satan points us away from his instigation of our ills and, instead, pits humans against each other and our loving God. Adam, the first man, answered God, "The woman whom thou gavest to be with me…" (Genesis 3:12 KJV), when asked what he had done. In essence, he blamed God and Eve for his own decision. Getting victims to blame victims and their Creator is Satan's greatest success. As my grandmother, Nettie, used to say, "He throws a rock and then hides his hand."

Racism is as certainly a demonic device, as is lying or stealing, but I am getting ahead of myself. I wasn't ready to hear any explanation for my hurt and disappointment. The racial wounds from childhood and adolescence had been ripped open, and the pain I felt was too searing. I retreated to the anger that I felt most comfortable with from my past.

I sought reasons to support my apostasy, and they were easy to find. I found a quote from one of our church founders that talked about slaves. It conveyed a sentiment about enslaved African Americans which I felt was racist and one that many 19th-century Whites had harbored. It ran against my sense of justice and fairness, and I took it personally. I sought answers from respected members of the church, pastors, and elders, but none could explain what she had written to my satisfaction. My righteous indignation was stoked; my mind was made up. The church was like the world I had grown up in, full of hypocrisy and broken promises.

I soon found other "good" reasons to distance myself from the faith I had once embraced so passionately. This person is doing this, and that person is doing that. People are hypocritical, and many other seemingly valid reasons filled my head. I am sure the devil was smiling all the while. Looking away from Christ to oneself or to others is one of the enemy's most successful tricks. Yet we do it all the time. I am reminded of Peter as he walked on the water. He looked away from Jesus and immediately began to sink. So, it was with me.

CHAPTER 3

The Journey into a Far Country

✝ *How did you go bankrupt?... Two ways...*
Gradually, then suddenly.[3]

—ERNEST HEMINGWAY

L ike that quote from the Hemingway novel *The Sun Also Rises,*
my spiritual bankruptcy was gradual, then sudden. The die was
cast, and the fire that had burned so fervently in my breast became an ember. Only God's grace and the prayers of the saints would keep
it from completely going out.

Although I found myself drifting into the deep waters of adulthood, I would keep the shore in view. The friends I had made and the lifestyle I had grown accustomed to felt comfortable to me. I could not abandon it all at once. And I wasn't the only one drifting. So many of my school friends were in the same boat as I was. Some of my friends who were raised in the church began to question their faith also. Young adulthood was a time of uncritical exploration for many of us and that exploration often led away from the values we were taught and believed.

Still, some entered the adult world firmly grounded in the church. Several encouraged me to do likewise. Donna Smith, a niece of Jacob Justiss, my former high school teacher, was one of them. She was a stalwart friend, and she, along with James "Slim" Davis, were roller-skating buddies. Donna in particular would often challenge me. "What if you're wrong and the Bible is right?" she would ask and, although I had a ready retort, her question stayed with me. There were others also, like Jonathan Watkins and Roosevelt Rayford, but they were fighting a losing battle. The world's siren call was too strong. Both Jonathan and Roosevelt wandered from the SDA Church's teaching and fell back into former habits.

Wilson Pickett's song lyrics "Don't let the green grass fool you," expressed the sentiment perfectly. Often what you think is good is not good for you. When away from home and the restraining influence of parents, the world, or more precisely the devil, offers so many enticements. Although we see the results of sin in the lives of the rich and famous all around us, their shattered lives, early deaths, and wasted potential, still like the rodents of the Pied Piper of Hamelin, we march blindly onward toward the same precipice.

One by one my friends began to settle down and get married. Many of the unions were unlikely fits, and most would end in divorce. Botts, Stewart, Chris, Andre, and Artie all tied the knot. Another close friend of mine at the time, Berval, told me that he was making a lot of bad business decisions, and marriage would help him correct that! I looked at Berval in disbelief but didn't argue with him. He had not mentioned love at all. The compounding of years, I discovered, did not make us any wiser, just older. I wasn't ready for marriage, and I knew it.

I felt more fortunate than some of my close friends, though. At least I had a college degree. In 1981, I started graduate school to major in industrial organizational psychology, but I just did not have the drive or passion I once had. I took some classes at George Mason University and then got a job as an aide on a psych ward at a renowned psychiatric hospital. Chestnut Lodge was a world-renowned facility in Montgomery County that catered to the wealthy and famous. Many of my college friends worked there. I worked there for nearly three years, while trying to find my way in life.

It was a good job with good benefits, and I enjoyed it. But I wanted more. I wanted to make money, to have a big house on the water, and to own a yacht. I would go to the marina in Southwest D.C. and look at the yachts and dream. I became restless. The siren song of the world cast a spell over me, and little by little I began to venture further from the shore of safety. I made new friends, some with unsavory reputations who wanted to make "quick" money, as I did. I was on a road I would never have selected to travel, but I was blinded by greed and selfishness. The Bible warns that "the love of money is the root of all evil" (1 Timothy 6:10 KJV), but the devil is subtle in his machinations.

The problem with temptation is that we only see the good side, and we minimize the bad consequences. One small step at a time will most as certainly take you to perdition as will a gallop. One small compromise leads to the next and then to the next, until the final leap becomes inconsequential. At least that's what you realize once it's too late. Then with success comes the accolades of others, the prestige, and the material benefits. The process is underway then suddenly you realize, you deserved it all along.

You have worked for it, hard. You have earned it, and never mind how you earned it. The world doesn't care so why should you?

As I reflect on those years, I tremble. I know for certain, and let me say that again with emphasis, I know for certain that it was only the Lord that saved me from prison or, worse yet, death. I could diverge and tell you many things, but I will simply say that "But for the grace of God, there go I." I will also add that the prayers of the righteous, in this case my mother, availeth much (see James 5:16). You will never be able to convince me that prayer doesn't work.

My Soulmate

People often ascribe fortuitous events to luck or chance. I'm not one of those people. In fact, I have taken those words out of my vocabulary. They are nonsensical for Christians. Some things that happen in life are ordained by God. What happened to me in the autumn of 1982 is one of those providences. I ran into one of the trio of friends I rode to college with; Cassandra and her sister, Sylvia, at Landover Mall. I was a salesman at the Luskin's Appliance and Electronics store there. Cassandra was all "grown-up," and she was beautiful! We talked briefly and exchanged phone numbers. In November of that year, we went on a date, but she was also dating a med student.

When I got to her house, I was surprised to see her sitting at the dining room table with several of her girlfriends. I knew them all, as most of them had gone to Oakwood. Cassandra was dressed plainly, while I had on my best "date night" outfit. I thought it strange, but wouldn't find out until later what the real story was. After our first date, she called me and gave me the "Dear John" spiel over the phone. I thought that was the end, until she called me the following February and asked me out!

"Hello, Nathaniel. Surprised to hear from me?"

"Yes, I am surprised. How are you doing?" My response was measured.

She continued. "I'm good. How are you?"

"Good." I wasn't sure where this was going and I wasn't going to extend myself.

"I thought about our first date. I had a good time. It brought back old memories."

I replied. "Yes, it did. I enjoyed it too."

"I also thought about our conversation after that. I guess you must have wondered what was wrong with me?" I did but I didn't tell her that. My silence prompted her to continue. "Well, I just wanted to make up for that. I'd like to take you out on another date and I will treat!"

I hesitated but accepted. "Okay. What happened to the guy you were dating?" I needed to know before I took the deep dive.

"We both agreed that our relationship wasn't working. We are still friends but nothing more. So, is this weekend good for you?"

I noticed how quickly she changed the subject and I didn't press the matter.

"Yes, that works. Let's check out a movie."

"That sounds good."

I was shocked, but I wasn't going to look a gift horse in the mouth. Our first time out was an ice cream parlor date and I spent nearly $8! Yes, I kept count. The next date was on Cassandra and I would hold her to it. Movies were more expensive than ice cream, so I would at least recover what I'd sunk on our first date.

She was true to her word, and she being a cheapskate that meant a lot. She and her friends later revealed to me that on our first date, when they were all gathered around the dining room table, she'd had second thoughts about going out and that she'd wanted to cancel but didn't have the heart. They told her to "dress down" so I would lose interest. It didn't work!

We dated for the next five years until we got married. We had our ups and downs and were engaged for a full year, but there was no doubt that she was the girl for me. I can honestly say that I am who I am today because God graced me with Cassandra. Her prayers would be added to my mom's, and God was in the midst of them both. Amen!

By the time I got married in October of 1987, I had committed to a career in real estate. In fact, it was on our honeymoon cruise that I decided to get my broker's license. Working a traditional job was something I found very difficult to do. Honestly, I had a hard time taking orders, especially from White people. I'd had a couple of run-ins with supervisors that did not end well, the last one culminating with me being escorted from the premises by two security guards. That was enough of that. I did not want to continue down that same path. So, real estate it was.

Real estate allowed me the freedom I needed to maintain my independence and sanity. However, the money, although good, had its ebbs and flows. My wife weathered the storms with grace, but I knew it was difficult for her. In 1991, I started my own business, Premier Appraisal Group, and bought my first home shortly after that. We had two daughters, Alexandra and Xavian, and were well into our version of the American dream. Cassandra was firmly in the church, and I was still searching for the all-elusive truth. I was thirty-five years old. More than fifteen years had passed since my first conversion and baptism, but the roller coaster ride still had some surprises for me.

The Baby Blessing

DuPont Park Seventh-day Adventist Church was a familiar place, and I knew many people who attended there. My in-laws were still members, and Cassandra was also. To my best recollection, I came to church that day for the baby blessing of my oldest daughter, Alexandra. Truthfully, I only vaguely remember the preacher. What I do remember is the subject he spoke about. He correlated the struggle of African Americans and social justice to the Christian struggle. He spoke eloquently about the injustices done to Black people in this country and how it should not be tolerated. He married the two controversies into one righteous cause, and he gave license to the belief that my struggle as a Black man was part and parcel of the Christian struggle. He emphasized that American social justice and the Christian ethic should not be separated. It reminded me of the late sixties, my impressionable years, when the Black power struggle had vibrancy.

I had never heard a sermon like his in a Seventh-day Adventist church. It moved me in a way that would change my perspective on America and my relation to her for the next part of my life. His sermon made me think about God's perfect timing. Ever since I had wandered away from the church, which at one time had filled me with purpose and passion, I had been looking for something to fill the void in my life. I was hungry for the truth, and for me to find it that day in church seemed like an act of God. This was a different "gospel," than the one I'd embraced at first. I was bewitched by the new narrative of social justice, forgetting that God's justice incorporates complete and perfect justice.

After this encounter with "social justice" Christianity and African American history, I began to study what I had been taught in the public school system and what I had learned through my experiences. I had to bring resolution to the hypocrisy and outright lies taught to me by the media and American history books, and I needed to make sense of the contradictions of my experience. Africans and Africans in America had made

scant contributions to civilization and society. That's what I've been educated to believe. Our absence in history books and television, especially in
westerns and dramas had been a puzzlement to me as a child. I could no
longer live with the insanity of it all. I needed to look off the beaten path
for truth that reconciled the two. What better place to start a search than
at a bookstore?

My Alma Mater was books, a good library...[4]

—*Malcolm X*

Caravan Books and Imports, run by a Muslim brother, was an African
American bookstore at a shopping center near my house. I went there
and browsed through his large selection of books for a good while. One
caught my eye. It was *Nile Valley Contributions to Civilization* by Anthony
Browder. This was not a typical history book. It was colorful, with loads
of seducing photos, and it was graphically pleasing. I would later find out
that the author had experience in graphic design, and he intentionally
made the book like that to entice buyers. It worked! The book was like an
archaeological dig for me. I had always been a student of history, but the
history I was taught had always been from a European perspective. Even
though the book discussed Egypt, Browder used a term I had never heard
before: "Kemet, the land of the Blacks."[5] Wow! In the time of the Pha-
raohs, Egypt was populated by Black people. That was a novel supposition.
The movies, like *Cleopatra* and *The Ten Commandments*, with Elizabeth
Taylor as Cleopatra and Charlton Heston as Moses, were just European
propaganda designed to steal hope from a people oppressed by centuries
of chattel slavery. This was my new enlightened revelation.

A sentiment attributed to Winston Churchill implies that part of the spoils
of victory is the privilege of writing the history books the way you desire.
This is an accurate account of western culture. Browder's history was dif-

ferent. It asked different questions and entertained different conclusions. It offered a different perspective on world events, one that was logical and meaningful to me, an oppressed African American. I was thirsty for more. Browder's book stretched my thinking and expanded my horizons. The lies that he exposes about African culture made me reexamine my entire belief system. He cites reputable sources, learned men from all over the world. Cheikh Anta Diop, Ivan Van Sertima, and Theophile Obenga were just a few of the authors that graced my expanding library. My appetite for this new information was insatiable. One by one, I began to buy and read their books. I discovered that the history I had learned in school never told the whole story. Significant details were left out or manipulated so as not to tarnish American mythology. *Lies My Teacher Told Me*, a book written by James W. Loewen, a White historian, provided additional legitimacy for my quest. With supporting facts, Loewen substantiates the American history lies that Jacob Justiss had also revealed to me so many years before.

The information that I was reading helped me answer questions that had long puzzled me about the world and how it got to be as it was. How had Europeans come to dominate the world? How had 10 percent of the world's population become the elite in such a short span of time? How had Black people, who were so talented in every walk of life, become the rump of humanity? There was a profound injustice about the state of world affairs, and now I thought I could finally get to the root of it. Another seed had been planted, and I would nourish it with my very life's energy. I found a new direction and a new purpose.

Since I was self-employed as a real estate broker and appraiser, I had the freedom of flexible work hours. I had other appraisers and agents working for my business, so this gave me the opportunity to study, even during the day. With free time on my hands, I thought about writing a book. It was something I had wanted to do in my 20s, but at the time I felt I didn't have enough life experiences. Now, I had gained those experiences, and I had a reason to write.

CHAPTER 4

Conspiracy Theories

✝ *Do not call conspiracy everything this people calls a conspiracy,*
do not fear what they fear, and do not dread it.

—ISAIAH 8:12 NIV

My life had been an unrelenting and unresolved search for understanding and reconciliation of the discordance in me and around me. In my search for peace I'd looked into religion, psychology, and history without success. Those had been surface explorations. Maybe it was time to dig deeper. Maybe it was time to discover for myself what was and what wasn't, what mattered and what didn't. The need to understand drove me forward as I pondered the idea of writing a book. Perhaps writing would help me uncover truths that would strengthen me and fortify me for life's inevitable trials and tribulations. Perhaps writing would quell the dust storm of lies that had so effectively blinded me from seeing my calling. It was time to take the next step and find out.

But what would I write about? I wasn't sure of my topic. I wasn't sure of the writing and publishing process either. I was certain of my feelings and their need for expression. All those things made me more than a little reluctant, and so I kept the idea to myself until I watched the brutal police beating of a Black man who was a few years younger than me. As I sat alone and silently watched the violent scene unfold on my color television screen, the trauma of similar scenes I had witnessed earlier as a child flooded back.

Four White police officers beat a defenseless Rodney Glen King as he pleaded for mercy. He was stunned with 50,000 volts of electricity and struck over 50 times with batons.[6] It confirmed what Annie Mae had said so many years before when she exposed me to the Book of Revelation. I had nearly forgotten what she said, but the horrific scene brought back her words in stark terms. *America is a beast*! Her actions nullify her words. The hypocrisy, I held to be self-evident. However, unlike the time when Annie Mae first spoke them to me, I didn't question the contradiction. Lamblike with a dragon's voice, that act of brutality was all the confirmation I needed. Racism and police brutality were not confined to the South, nor were they a bygone phenomenon. In its treatment of Black people, America had not changed, nor I concluded would it ever. The Bible prophecy was right. Life has a strange way of repeating itself. As a child I questioned God and waited for His answer; as a man I questioned myself and took matters into my own hands. Waiting for God to answer had not worked before, so I thought; I wouldn't chance that disappointment again.

Los Angeles erupted after the acquittal of those four White policemen. The anger at injustice I felt as a child had now matured into a full-blown rage at a patently unjust and unholy system. I had been gifted my topic on a silver screen platter. As a child the questions incited by a racist culture were difficult to formulate, but as a man, I articulated my hypothesis with a clear purpose. What was the worldwide conspiracy against Black people? Who was behind it and what was their purpose? How could we stop them from killing us? What would we need and who could we count on?

The Genocide Files would explain the process and answer each of the questions I had posed. That was my book's title, and it also became my mission. It would attempt to explain the world conspiracy against Black people. To make the book as historically accurate as I could, I found myself researching 44 books on topics ranging from contemporary Brazilian culture to Ice Age European archaeology. Based on the response from my reading public, it was a task well worth the effort. The book was a mystery-action novel that was perfect for a big screen adaptation.

The Genocide Files

The plot of the book revolves around the two main characters—Matthew Peterson and Ewanikee Briscoe. Although both are African American, they are from very different backgrounds. Matt, an orphan, was brought up in elite, White America. A wealthy patron saw to his every need. He attended the best prep schools and learned how to live as a successful, Black man in wealthy, White America. American racism was something he had read about, but it was not anything he had experienced, at least that is what he tells himself.

Proud of who she is, Ewanikee is a beautiful, intelligent, Black woman. A streetwise reporter, she knows how to mingle with all strata of people. In some ways, her background is like Matthew's. She was brought up in the inner city but with mentors who provided her guidance. She had grown up with a genuine compassion for the Black underclass and a hatred for those who made them so.

The connection that brings these two together is when Matthew, along with his partners, recently purchases the newspaper where Ewanikee works as a reporter. As the working partner, Matthew needs to learn the insides of what makes the paper successful, and it is also something that he wants to do to learn more about who he is. He hasn't figured out the best approach to get started, and then an opportunity presents itself.

The infamous "Christmas Murders," the name given the killings by the newspapers in a suburb of Chicago, is a gift on a silver platter and it is what brings Matthew and Ewanikee into immediate contact. Matthew is heading home from a Christmas Eve party when the police radio band in his car alerts him to a disturbance. He is one of the first on the scene in a tranquil, suburban Chicago enclave.

An entire family has been murdered, execution style. The husband was a police officer who had been tied to the highly politicized murder of a Black activist several years before. What Matthew and Ewanikee uncover lead to the discovery of a secret society known only as "Triangle." Triangle has a worldwide presence, particularly on the continents of Africa and both North and South America. This is the triangle, much like the slave trade triangle. The pair discovers that the men and women of Triangle are not interested in politics or social change through traditional and accepted methods. No, the Triangle plan is simple. It is to take back what had been so violently and ruthlessly taken from them. Triangle has the numbers, they have the plan, and they have the will. That is what makes them dangerous. In a short time, Matthew finds out just how dangerous Black pragmatists with a plan and a purpose can be.

Matthew and Ewanikee discover the genocide files themselves. The files had been secreted away from a government sponsored "think tank," and they are comprehensive down to the smallest detail. The files cover every aspect of human interaction—from A to Z. Nothing has been left out, and the plan is ruthless, with the stated goal of elimination of most of the world's population of color. From the perspective of Triangle, there really isn't much choice—it is survival or extinction. Also, from their perspective, the full title of Darwin's book says it all, and lays out the intention of the modern European power structure: *On the Origin of Species by Means of Natural Selection, or the Preservation of Favoured Races in the Struggle for Life.* That is the conspiracy spelled out for the whole world to see.

The Genocide Files is a work of fiction, but it was fomented in the factual practices of American slavery and American eugenics, the latter which inspired Hitler and fed Nazi racism. The scientific malfeasance of the Tuskegee syphilis experiment, along with other atrocities, were the real-world genocide files. Too often, in the world that Black people inhabit, conspiracy theories collide with reality, and it becomes maddening and virtually impossible to determine the truth from the lie. *The Genocide Files* makes clear what was truth and what were lies. It defines who the good guys were and who the bad guys were. Its black and white simplicity was the root cause of its success. It looks the enemy in the eye and does not blink.

Finding My Voice

I finally mentioned to a few family members my intention to write a book, but only my brother-in-law, Dennis Smith, took me seriously. I started writing the book in September of 1996, and it was completed in roughly a year's time. By the fall of the next year, 1997, I was a published author. My opening event was held on an October Sunday, on 8th Street on Capitol Hill. The shop was a quaint gallery with books, picture-framing, and art, and with the perfect clientele for the promotion. The book signing was a great success. Many people turned out, including a couple of reporters from local newspapers. Great reviews came in, and the book garnered a cult following.

Who would have thought this would happen? I had been too young to participate when the civil rights movement swept the South in the era of Martin and Malcolm. I was a child, of course, but still I had wanted to do something. With so many others, I stood safely on the sidelines and watched White America sic dogs and unleash water hoses on people that looked like me. The images of government sanctioned terrorism were seared into my young psyche. When Martin Luther King Jr. was assassinated, I stood on the top step at the concrete apron of our home's sidewalk in Southeast D.C. and watched the orange glow of a city on fire light the skyline. I was terrified, yet hopeful. I thought, "Is this how the world ends?" I was 11-years-old.

In those turbulent years of the '60s, America changed, but not enough and not really. The colors on the American flag were the same as those on the Confederate flag. The pattern of racism was different, but the design was exactly the same—subjugation of African Americans. So, it was in American society—north or south, east or west, liberal or conservative. Labels don't change people—labels only categorize them. That is what Triangle, the Pan-Africanist secret society in my book, understood—White supremacy is racism plain and simple and it was not acceptable.

Now, with *The Genocide Files*, I had raised my voice in protest, along with the torches of those who had set my youthful world on fire. I was amazed at how many people the book touched and how it provoked the same feelings and desires in them that I had felt compelled to put into words. I met so many angry and frustrated people, people who felt hopeless in the land of promise. In their eyes America had betrayed them and would never fulfill its word to them or to their children. My book gave voice to their angst and emboldened me. As I wrote each page, my mission came more into focus. I was surprised by how easily the words and the storyline formed inside my mind. I had read how difficult it is for writers. The infamous "writers block" was something I feared, but it never happened to me. I wrote daily and with enthusiasm.

In retrospect, I understand why. But as so often happens in life, the road you choose doesn't always lead you to the place you want to be. This was just the beginning of my foray into the quicksand of American racial politics, and it would have twists and turns that even the heroes of my fictional novel could not have anticipated. The racial controversy was real, but it was not what I thought it was, nor were the players so easily identified as I had been educated to think. I thought I knew who the real players were and who the pawns were. I thought I knew what the objectives were and how they would be achieved. Finally, I thought I knew what my role was in the grand scheme of things. I was sorely mistaken on all points!

CHAPTER 5

Roots Public Charter School

✝ *If you can control a man's thinking you do not have to worry about his action. When you determine what a man shall think you do not have to concern yourself about what he will do. If you make a man feel that he is inferior, you do not have to compel him to accept an inferior status, for he will seek it himself. If you make a man think that he is justly an outcast, you do not have to order him to the back door. He will go without being told; and if there is no back door, his very nature will demand one.*[7]

—CARTER G. WOODSON

*S**hortly after I got the idea for** my book, I started attending a study group in Northwest D.C. The group was named in honor of Kwame Nkrumah, the first Prime Minister of Ghana, who had led his country to independence from British rule in 1957. The study group was aptly named. It had a cross-section of people from all walks of life. I was one of the youngest members, and I felt honored to be among my enlightened Elders.

Kamau Robinson was a teacher at the school. He was "Black and proud" with shoulder length locks and a magnetic personality. Kamau was only a few years older than me, but he had a wealth of knowledge. He also had a quick wit and a ready smile. I still fondly recall a saying or two that I learned from him. There was one statement that he used often, which was coined by Neely Fuller, and it summed up his philosophy. It went something like this, and it explained the reason we were all there:

Unless you understand White supremacy, what it is and how it works, everything else you "think" you know will only serve to confuse you.

This was more than an expression. It was the guiding principle behind the need for total re-education. This was the hand, holding the rope, pulling us out of the quicksand of White cultural dominance. Like many of the other members of the group, I held on for dear life. The statement underscored the fact that, without proving it first, African Americans could not trust anything in this country as it pertained to the wellbeing of Black people. The Tuskegee experiments, Rosewood, Tulsa, Wilmington, Emmett Till, the eugenics movement, these were just a few of the living examples that were transcribed into our corporate DNA. White supremacy was the boogey man that stalked us in broad daylight. Kamau exemplified this attitude with extreme prejudice. I admired him for it.

Then there was Asagai, Gerald Smith, who was well known in D.C.'s African American cultural circles. For some time, he had been a regular on the Cathy Hughes radio station, WOL, and was always ready for a verbal

altercation. He was brilliant and a lecturer in his own right. Erriel Rob-
erson was a young man with a bright future as well as a member of the
group. He was in his 20s and had already written a couple of books on
African American culture. Erriel had insight well beyond his years. He
was also a sought-after speaker and a genuinely nice guy. He and I would
become fast friends.

There were others in the group as well, many who were current or former
United States government workers. All of them had stories of systematic
racism, some so blatant that I found them hard to believe. After I had
shown my awe and disbelief of their plaintive stories a few times, I learned
to contain my angst to avoid ridicule. On any given Wednesday night
when we met, there would be ten to fifteen people in attendance. The older men there were called "Baba" and, as I recall, the title for older women
was "Nana."

From time to time, well-known authors would grace our meetings. Tony
Browder did a lecture series for the group and was profoundly informa-
tive. Dr. Marimba Ani was one of my favorites. She had written *Yurugu*,
a scholarly work of over six hundred pages, which was a favorite at that
time and had a large following. Its critique of European culture was mesmerizing. Dr. Ani had spent time in Africa when she wrote *Yurugu*, and
she shared from both an African and Afro-American cultural perspective.
She resembled my grandmother, and I told her so. Her response was, "We
might be related. You just don't know in this country."

The study always started with a libation to the ancestors, which I considered the most unusual of practices and one I did not feel quite comfortable
with at first. However, it seemed normal to everyone else in attendance.
Being the newest member of the group, I didn't want to be the odd man
out, so I joined in with as much enthusiasm as I could muster. From this,
I learned that whether we recognize it or not, almost everything we do as

human beings has a religious or worship component to it. This is the bedrock of our existence. We are hardwired to worship someone or something.

I was learning so much. It was a natural high without drugs, just knowledge. All of this new knowledge felt very natural to me. My negative reaction to White racism was a natural and almost instinctive response. As I studied, it began to make sense to me. The people in the group, by sharing their experiences so intimately, helped me come to terms with my own feelings. The anger and hatred I had was a protective response to the brutality and terrorism I had experienced. We fed off each other, and our shared sentiments were rarely challenged no matter how radical they were. A friend and member of DuPont Park Seventh-day Adventist Church, Herbert Buchanan, started attending some of the meetings with me, and he added his stories about government racism to our catalog. He had retired from the U.S. Government Printing Office and had many stories of his own.

Ours was an eclectic blend of spiritual disciplines, much like I had grown up with. Yoga, Reiki, meditation, and martial arts were all practiced by various members of the group. The list was much longer, but you get the picture. I also began to view all of these things from a different perspective. To those who understood their origins, the practices were all cultural, and all culture had originated in Africa. *The Mis-Education of the Negro* was not just a book, it was a process of physical and mental enslavement from which we were duty bound to free ourselves.

My indoctrination had been comprehensive, but what I failed to recognize was the spiritual roots of each practice. That part was hidden from me by my true enemy. The problem was clear. I felt if you were not part of the solution, you were indeed part of the problem. I wanted to be part of the solution, and so when a group was formed as a think tank to address the problems of enslaved African Americans, I was asked to join. The year was 1999. Some of the members of the group were well-known authors and speakers. Again, I felt honored. I had an office on Capitol Hill at that time, and that was the address of our first meeting. My office was a rowhouse that I had converted into office space. As I recall, Browder, Ani, Asagai, and Erriel were all part of the think tank group.

There were others, some of whom I knew by name and others by reputation. I pulled out the red carpet for my guests, and I felt people were impressed with the building and its accoutrements. Everyone was polite and complimentary of one another. Once all the pleasantries were attended to, we performed a libation and a prayer. By then, I had grown quite accustomed to the ritual.

As we opened the first meeting, one of the striking moments was a prayer given by a young woman. I don't recall her name. The prayer was not to any god I knew, but it was thoughtful and mesmerizing, almost like a spell. Others in the room commented on it after she had finished. She related a story that illustrated the context of the prayer. The story was rich with indigenous African cultural meaning. It seemed we would never stop learning about our stolen heritage.

We decided on a name for the group. I cannot recall the full name, but Maafa was part of it. Maafa, which meant "great disaster" in Swahili and represented the plight of the African Diaspora, was the central expression that the group name was to convey. It was the African Holocaust, which had lasted for centuries.

Little by little, I was being exposed to a world that I understood very little about, a world that appeared to be one way on its surface, but was another underneath. It was a world that held out beautiful promises of personal and cultural discovery and mental emancipation, but it was one, I would find, that had neither the plan nor the ability of fulfilling those promises. It would be a hard lesson, and one that I would never forget.

On a basic level, all of us in the group had similar experiences. Our common pain would glaze over the differences among us. We had, in common, the anger and angst directed at a country and culture that penalized us for simply "being." These were the same feelings my friends and I felt while we were growing up. Age and insight had just made me more frustrated by the suffocating noose around my neck.

The Genocide Files allowed me to express that anger in a constructive way, by venting my emotions through the pages of a work of fiction. But pain and trauma that spans generations and continents requires more than venting. It requires a medicine that is not manufactured. Only God can heal those hurts. Only God can apply the balm that will mend those wounds. I didn't know it at that time, but I would begin to understand what so many of my African American heroes had learned before me.

I had met some of them and sat on discussion panels. I had spoken to them in private and heard their melancholy opining on a struggle whose victory seemed always out of reach. Some of them had spent their entire lives yelling against the societal waves of prejudice and racism, only to leave footprints on a sandy beach with high tide approaching. Some had shed their lifeblood in protests and marches without any tangible or measurable rewards. As I listened to their regrets and felt their disillusionment, I began to understand the futility of the struggle. I had begun to feel the same way, yet I always suppressed my doubts and continued on the same path. Their voiced discontent made my concerns audible, although without resolution. My experiences would open a door of wisdom that would spare me from their discouragement and fate. I share with you some of those experiences now.

The Bureau of Alcohol, Tobacco, and Firearms

Hakim, a tall, lean, dark-skinned and regal man, who owned Caravan Books and Imports, asked me to do a lecture and book signing one Saturday afternoon. The store was in the Rivertown Commons Shopping Center in Oxon Hill, Maryland. I agreed, and we met at the store on an early autumn day, under a cerulean sky. There were 15 to 20 people in attendance, which was all that the store could comfortably accommodate. Men and women were present, and we had a very lively discussion. I would read passages from my book and then give an author's insight on the text. The book often stirred up passions in readers, and that was the case at this meeting. Consequently, our discussions got lengthy.

Finally, as the group dismissed, some of the attendees browsed the store, while others just casually talked. This was nothing unusual at book signings. Eventually, the next-to-last attendee left, and Hakim and I were still talking. A young man, who had attended the lecture but hadn't said anything, drew our attention. That was his intention. He introduced himself and asked to speak to me. Again, I did not think too much of it as this often happened when people wanted more information about the novel.

However, this time was different. Hakim and I sat down, and the young man followed suit and introduced himself. He told us that he was a sniper with the ATF (the Bureau of Alcohol, Tobacco, Firearms and Explosives). Under normal circumstances, that information was not something he would readily disclose. He had our attention. He looked the part; clean-cut and muscular, with a matter-of-fact air about him. As he pulled out his identification, I began to feel uncomfortable, not sure of where our conversation was heading. By the uncertain glance Hakim gave me, I could see that he was also uncomfortable. He spoke candidly.

"As I mentioned, I work for the ATF. My girlfriend read your book and suggested that I read it too. She actually did more than suggest. When she passed it to me, the cover artwork and the title got my attention right off the bat. If you don't mind me asking, who did the artwork?"

"Michael Brown. Michael did the official poster for the Million Man March," I offered with a pinch of pride. "He did a great job." He could see that he had our undivided attention. He continued.

"First, let me say that I loved the book. It was a fantastic read. Once I picked it up, I couldn't put it down. The characters seemed so real and the plot is so plausible, especially with everything that's been happening lately. Secondly, let me say that you're not in any immediate danger, but your book, for lack of better words, has been placed on a watch list. The part about the ATF hit too close to home for some people at the agency."

He was referencing a recent event involving the ATF. I fictionalized a real event that had occurred in Virginia, one which had received unfavorable publicity. At that event, some of the officers had worn KKK paraphernalia and paraded around with a hangman's noose. The real incident happened right before the book was published. I responded to him.

"Yes, I read about that in the newspaper. I think it was the *Post.* I couldn't believe it when I read it, so I included it for dramatic effect."

He continued. "Well, it worked. You definitely got some people's attention. Let me just say, your book, *The Genocide Files,* is perceived as a threat in some circles. It has a grassroots appeal, and that makes it dangerous."

I looked at Hakim and he looked back at me. I tried to shrug off his comments with a show of "Oh, well" bravado, but I was concerned. Hakim had an uncertain look on his face as he then shared a personal experience that happened back in the '70s. Hakim gave us the short version.

"When I became a Muslim, me and a group of guys I grew up with, we were involved in some protests and political activism. We were serious about changing the power structure and real outspoken about it, but as you get older, things change and you quiet down some. When I, when we, tried to get jobs, government jobs, we couldn't. It was strange, none of us were able to get into the government. We suspected that we were on some type of list. It wasn't unusual either—we'd heard about government "watch lists" from others we knew. That's why I'm in business for myself. I had to find a way to provide for my family."

There was silence for a moment. The young man took a deep breath before finishing.

"Well, let me say again, you have a great book. I wish you success with it. Take care of yourself and your family." As we parted ways, we all stood. I decided to leave too; what more could I say. The conversation put me in a reflective mood. His last words rang loudly in my mind. "Take care of yourself and your family."

As I drove home, my exercise in protest suddenly took on a new dynamic. I had never thought about not being able to work or run my business because of government harassment, but this conversation changed it all. My naiveté was being stripped away, and although it was a painful process, it was necessary. A short time later, while in my front driveway, I noticed a "device" I'd never seen before on a street light near my house. It had an antenna on it that pointed downward. I brought it to my wife's attention. The juxtaposition of the ATF agent and its sudden appearance was worth noting. Was I being paranoid? Paranoia is a legitimate response under some circumstances, mine was one.

In my research for this book, I would learn how deep this government paranoia went. You cannot throw gasoline on a fire and not expect to feel the heat. My own research into COINTELPRO (Counter Intelligence Program) should have been a warning to me of how far the American government would go to persecute dissidents. After all, this was the America where protest often ended in false imprisonment or death. I had too many examples not to realize it, but I had not written my book for that purpose. I had just written a mystery novel, a work of fiction. The powers that be, did they take these things so seriously? Again, I had cited too many examples in my book to dismiss what I knew to be a resounding yes! The ATF agent's words of warning rang true, and I knew I had crossed a line. Was it too late to turn around? I wasn't sure if it was or even if I wanted to. It seemed that I was going deeper into the rabbit hole than I felt comfortable with. My next encounter would change my thinking and seal my attitude.

Black Power

My publicist had gotten a call from a group in Forestville who thought the book should have as wide a circulation as possible. They wanted me to speak and do a book signing. I agreed. Forestville had several business districts with small warehouses and housing-trade related shops. Having previously lived nearby, I was familiar with the general area. Still, there were parts of Forestville that I had not visited. The book signing would take place in one of those places.

As I pulled up to the business address, the parking lot was nearly full. There were several motorcycles and what we grew up calling "muscle" cars. There were other cars there as well. I got out of my car, not sure what to expect, but I was pleasantly surprised. One of the benefits of notoriety was the respect and attention lavished by one's patrons. The group was comprised of young, Black men, probably twenty of them or so. They took the book and what it advocated very seriously. The president of the group greeted me warmly and took me to where I would be sitting in the front. As I recall, that meeting was on a Sunday.

The shop was clean and well decorated with a lot of the colors black, red, and green. It was more like a clubhouse, with pictures and Afrocentric memorabilia on the walls. Everyone was respectful. I got comfortable and read a passage or two from the book. We began to discuss them. The president of the group spoke first.

"Mr. Arnold, your book is so timely. I mean, you're talking about things that are happening right now!"

I replied, "Thanks. Much of what I talk about in the book are real world experiences."

"We've done a lot of studying ourselves too. The think tanks and COINTELPRO, those are facts. The way you put it together makes so much sense. Ewanikee is a bad sister. This would make a great movie and it would influence a lot of our people."

"I think so," was my reply.

Another young man chimed in. "Sir, the Triangle organization: Is there anything like that. I mean that you based your research on?"

I saw where he was going. "There have been groups and movements in history but none quite like Triangle, no."

Someone else added to the train of thought with emphasis. "Everyone in this room has had negative encounters with the police, everyone. I'm tired of it. Your book shows how police brutality should be handled, the only way it can be handled—deadly force against deadly force." The room agreed with him.

I listened as the men there began to tell their stories, their anger on full display. I'd had several run-ins with cops myself, so I could truly empathize. The president asked me a pointed question.

"Mr. Arnold, based on what you know, what would it take to do what your book talks about?"

I adjusted my seat before answering. "That's a good question. I'm not sure." What the ATF agent said was fresh in my mind. What I knew about COINTELPRO and its planting agents in groups like this was also fresh in my mind. I was careful not to say more. "It would take a lot of thought and planning."

I stopped as if I was in reflection. "It would take a lot."

The president of the group continued. "I'm not afraid of dying. I know what rights I have. White people didn't give them to me, they took them away. If we have to fight for them, that's fine. We train with firearms, everybody here, we know how to use them. Whatever happens, happens."

Heads and voices blended in agreement. I agreed with a head shake also.

It was clear what they wanted and I knew that I couldn't give it to them. I felt uncomfortable. They wanted to make Triangle a reality, not just an organization in a novel. They were the volunteers, and they wanted guidance and direction. I could not share with them what I had learned through writing the book or what I had begun to feel as I met with people during my book signings. What the ATF agent had said about my book's grassroots appeal, I was witnessing firsthand. I knew then why it would be considered a threat. I had learned, from calls and letters received by myself and my publicist, that the book had been banned in several state prisons and was being used in at least one western university.

As plausible as the book sounded, the premise was far removed from the reality. When I wrote it, I was moved by my years of indignation at an unjust system. The anger I felt was given an acceptable outlet, veiled in the guise of fiction. Using artistic license, I felt safe and shielded from the full brute force of American wrath. When writing I never thought beyond the moment and certainly not of being in the limelight of a movement. I remembered what Malcolm, Martin, and others in the struggle had experienced. I was not prepared for that; the sidelines suited me just fine after all. At most, I thought the storyline might make a good movie. But anything further than that, I had not given much thought to. Obviously, I needed to think again.

In doing my research for the book, I had gained a broader understanding of how conspiracies worked. From my, research I discovered that conspiracies are ingenious, diabolical, and deceptive. Deception was the central tenet to all of them, and we know that deception, by default, is evil. The

research I had done on COINTELPRO was a key example. COINTEL-
PRO was a United States government program developed to spy on and
immobilize Americans who disagreed with mainstream government poli-
cies, but especially Black people. It ignored the constitution and employed
various government agencies in the process of doing so. I discovered that,
at its height in the '60s, a full third of the people in some of the Black civil
rights organizations, were informants or on the COINTELPRO payroll.
Those organizations included the Black Panthers, the Nation of Islam, and
the Student Nonviolent Coordinating Committee, among others. The
very government that was charged to protect the rights of American citi-
zens was the same government that undermined their organizations, along
with their African American collaborators.

My historical research had also shown that in earlier times, conspiracies
worked the same way as in modern times. They were just as ingenious, diabolical, and deceptive. One such example was the Guy Fawkes, or Gunpowder Plot, in 1605, which was an attempt to assassinate King James I
of England and overthrow his government. That conspiracy is also very
relevant to our later discussions.

At that time, the Pope collaborated with a corps of Jesuit co-conspirators
to blow up the House of Lords during the state opening of Parliament on
November 5, 1605. Guy Fawkes, who had been a soldier in the Spanish
army, along with accomplices, smuggled thirty-six barrels of gunpowder
into the cellar directly below Parliament. It was enough to destroy the entire building and everyone in it. God intervened in this mass assassination
attempt by members of the Catholic Church. William Parker, a member
of Parliament and a Catholic himself, received an anonymous letter telling him not to attend the opening. Alarmed by the letter, he took it to
King James, who immediately had the basement searched. While being
tortured, Guy Fawkes revealed the sordid details of the plot and who was
involved. Even the Pope was implicated.

Had the Gunpowder Plot succeeded, it would have effectively decapitated the British government and much of its ruling class. The second phase of the plot was then to install a new government run by puppets of the Catholic Church and its followers. The Protestant movement in Britain would have been crippled and possibly even ended. We will never know what far reaching effects the successful plot might have had, but we do understand its purpose—unlawful Catholic hegemony in a sovereign nation!

My research opened my eyes to the Universal Church in a way it never had before. It also led me to the conclusion that disconnected groups, with seemingly divergent interests, will come together for a singular purpose, and that purpose is always the distribution of earthly power. The thirst for power is the lifeblood of all conspiracies—who has it, and who wants it. That is what makes conspiracies so diabolical and dangerous because it cuts across all party lines. Just look at America, and the world of today. Look at the battle lines drawn over Black and White, conservative and liberal, straight and gay, Black Lives Matter, the Me-Too movement, and the Common Good for climate change. At their central issue, these disparate movements all strive for the distribution of temporal power, to keep it themselves or deny it to others. Of course, so did all the movements before them: Jew versus Gentile, Catholic versus Protestant, Fascism, Marxism, and a nearly endless list of "isms." The titles may have been different, but the struggle was, and is, the same. That is what I understood about conspiracies at that time.

I have a different perspective now, along with a biblical understanding of how all conspiracies are tied together which came by the living and growing process—simply put, life. I leave my quote on what God has shown me relating to all conspiracies now.

Conspiracy theories result from our inability to fathom the abject depravity of sin, the power, character and malfeasance of its originator, the resultant evil and suffering it spawns on earth, in demons and men, and conversely our perplexity and disbelief of the beneficent character, the longsuffering nature, and love of our omnipotent Creator who in spite of sin seeks to save us.

—*Nathaniel Xavier Arnold*

My life circumstances changed my perspective about life and my direction. There are pivotal moments in life and I was about to have one of those moments. As is often the case, those moments come unexpectedly. My dramatic entrance to life's next phase was only a phone call away.

CHAPTER 6

Life Interrupts Living

✝ *I had fainted, unless I had believed to see the goodness of the
Lord in the land of the living.
Wait on the Lord: be of good courage, and he shall strengthen
thine heart: wait, I say, on the Lord.*

—PSALM 27:13-14 KJV

I t was a late February day in 2000. My doctor called me on my
home phone. Dr. Williams spoke in a calm, pleasant, but concerned
voice. I was in the kitchen when I answered. He began politely but
with not much small talk.

"Hello, Mr. Arnold. We got your test results back from the lab. We noticed some abnormalities in it."

I stammered, as a million thoughts raced through my head. "I'm sorry, what do you mean, abnormalities?"

"Well, Mr. Arnold, your white cell count is high—quite high in fact. We'd like to have you come in for additional testing."

"So, what do you think the problem is?"

"Well, it points to a chronic illness. It's called chronic lymphocytic leukemia."

I couldn't force myself to say the word cancer. I couldn't say anything at all.

"Mr. Arnold, are you still there?"

Through my shock, I replied. "Yes, I'm still here." There had to be another explanation. I continued. "I was just thinking I have bad allergies, really bad allergies, and it's that time of year when they start to flare up. I think that might have something to do with it."

It was too early in the year for spring allergies, but he didn't argue with me. "Well, the testing we want you to take will let us know for certain."

"Okay."

He finished. "Expect to hear from our office in a couple of weeks for additional testing. I know this is hard Mr. Arnold, but try not to worry."

"Thanks, I'll wait to hear from you all." As I hung up the phone my heart dropped to the floor. Trying not to worry was the least possible thing for me to do.

It took a moment, but after I'd pulled myself together, I told my wife what was going on. Of course, she was quite concerned. When I met with doctor Williams again, he confirmed I had chronic lymphocytic leukemia (CLL), but he seemed hopeful for my treatment and informed me that I'd need to see an oncologist to stage and treat the illness. I was not going to just sit still, though. I started researching what it was and how it could be treated. My brother, Ullysee, was in treatment for cancer at that time. Also, a family friend, Herbert Buchanan, would eventually die from an acute form of leukemia. I knew what they both had been going through, and I was scared.

Not long after that visit, I remember being in my office on Capitol Hill. It was early evening, but already dark and raining. As I looked out the office window, I thought, *Is this the end?* Then I fell to the floor, and with my face on the floor, I prayed to God, "Let me live!" I asked to see my daughters, grown and married. I did not want to die. I wanted to live, and I cried bitter tears. As I look back on that moment, I realize that it was my King Hezekiah experience.

It is times like these that help you to put things into perspective. All your dreams, aspirations, fears, and hopes melt into one single prayer: "Lord save me!" Nothing else matters. Nothing. So, what was I going to do? The Seventh-day Adventist health reform message was a good place to start. I went home and emptied my cabinets and refrigerator of junk food and refined sugar. I was committed to changing how I ate and what I ate. I started juicing and sought out a holistic, integrative doctor. I found one on Connecticut Avenue. I accomplished this all before the medical team had "staged" the cancer.

I read books on cancer and the various methods of treating it. I investigated meditation and deep breathing techniques. I wanted to get a head start on the disease and do what I could to increase the odds in my favor. In June, when we went to see the specialist, I was so nervous that I couldn't drive. My wife understood and drove us to his office in Greenbelt. Once we were there, the doctor explained to us the procedure and he administered anesthesia. After it took effect, about a half hour later, he took a bone marrow sample. That was it. A week later, we went back to his office for the results.

The cancer was stage one, which was good news. They had found abnormal T-cells, and this was confirmation that I did have cancer. Since I had no debilitating symptoms or pain, the doctor suggested that, for now, I wait and see how the cancer developed. I prayed a prayer of relief and recommitted myself to right eating and the integrative medical approach. I had not forgotten my prayer to God for healing, but I knew it was my responsibility to do my part, and I committed myself to change.

There was a restaurant called Everlasting Life on Georgia Avenue in D.C. Everlasting Life had a juice bar and served raw foods. My first time there, I looked at all the raw vegetable blends with their exotic names, and none of it seemed appealing. Daniel, my old friend from Hillcrest, walked up behind me wearing his fireman's uniform and gear, and we embraced. He told me what to try, and that was my first foray into all raw eating. The restaurant became a mainstay for me.

They also sponsored holistic seminars and brought in speakers from around the country. They held one such event at Howard University's Cramton Auditorium. Two of the presenters were medical doctors: Mona Harrison and Jewel Pookrum. Dr. Harrison had been traveling back and forth to Africa and was excited about certain herbs and other things that she had found there that she felt would revolutionize medicine in this country. As I listened to her lecture and later talked to her personally, I was excited too.

It was only a few months later that Dr. Harrison was found dead in Africa, under mysterious circumstances. That was a too familiar story in the circles we were in. Of course, people die all the time, but often, the fact that they are engaged in activities to help further the wellbeing of Black people makes their deaths suspicious. Paranoia runs deep in the African American community, and not without cause. There weren't many details on her death and that fed directly into the conspiracy theory surrounding it. There was nothing that could be done; death had the final say. I continued on my own journey.

Sebi the Healer

Sebi the healer was a personal friend of the owner of Everlasting Life and he was presenting an event at a venue in D.C. I had never heard of him before, but based on what I had been told, I thought he would be worth seeing. I wasn't having any negative symptoms with my health, but I wanted to be rid of the cancer altogether. Mr. Buchanan had died, and my brother's condition was up and down, so I was willing to try anything I could get to help. The thing is, there are many so-called "cures" for cancer, and everybody and their uncle wants to give advice. Most of it is well-meaning, but it is often contradictory. In many cases, even doctors don't agree on a course of treatment, and all of it comes with a price tag.

Sebi was a charismatic man who had a broad smile and engaging sense of humor. The people in the venue with me that afternoon were enthralled with his presentation. He had a young female assistant, Mananna, who was attentive to his every need. She was there to take orders and schedule appointments for personal visits. His theory on mucus as the root cause of all disease was novel to me, and I thought it worth it to do more research. So, after the meeting, I set up a one-on-one consultation. Sebi was staying in the area for a few days to hold consults with other patients. In fact, the hotel he had chosen was on Oxon Hill Road only a short distance from my house. At the venue, I also bought some of the herbal remedies he was selling. Without recommendation from my doctor, I started taking them.

I was fortunate that the day I met privately with Sebi was a light workday for him. His assistant was there when we met, and she handled the paperwork and the fees. Then, she left with a friend of mine who had also attended the meeting. It was around lunch time, and they went to get some food from a nearby restaurant. After they left, Sebi and I began to talk.

Sebi had a wealth of experience. He had been all over the country and parts of South America. Even though he had not been born here, he had fond memories of Mobile, Alabama, my hometown. Most of the experiences he shared involved a woman and marijuana, and he had a lot of them! Based on the stories he shared, I began having mixed feelings about him. At the event, I had an impression of Sebi as being the typical "holy" man, but after talking with him one-on-one for a good length of time, that impression changed.

I had an image in my head that a genuine healer would be a man of fealty to God because I believed that all healing came from God. In my spirit, I knew that unless God gave the order to heal someone, then all the herbs or medicine in the world would not cure them. God must give the order first, as in the case of King Hezekiah. Sometimes God uses things He has made to facilitate healing, again as in the case of King Hezekiah. He instructed him to make a poultice of figs, but that is not always the case.

By merely speaking to a sick person, Jesus and His disciples healed them according to their faith. In the case of the woman with the issue of blood, she simply touched Jesus' garment and she was healed, again by faith in God. Peter's shadow fell on others, and they were healed of their diseases. The Bible is full of instances like this, all related to faith in God. In the Gospel of John, chapter nine, Jesus and His disciples came across a blind man. Jesus used his saliva to make mud, which he then placed over the man's eyes. He then told the man to go to the pool of Siloam and wash the mud off. The blind man did as he was told, and to his great joy he could see! He then proclaimed his healing to those he knew and got the attention of the religious leaders of his day, the Pharisees. He was brought before the Pharisees for questioning.

Because of their prejudices, the Pharisees refused to believe that he had been born blind and that he had been healed. They condemned Jesus for healing the man on the sabbath and called in the man's parents. They questioned the parents, and were told that the man had indeed been born blind, but the Pharisees refused to believe his parents also. So, they called in the man again and questioned him further. This is what he told them:

The man answered and said unto them, Why herein is a marvellous thing, that ye know not from whence he is, and yet he hath opened mine eyes. Now we know that God heareth not sinners: but if any man be a worshipper of God, and doeth his will, him he heareth. Since the world began was it not heard that any man opened the eyes of one that was born blind. If this man were not of God, he could do nothing.

—*John 9:30–33 KJV*

The truth stated here is simply this: the Creator God is the God of all healing. All healing comes from Him. He doesn't share His healing power with those who do not belong to Him. To understand this principle, you only need to read this biblical account once. Anybody who claims to be able to heal you and who is not of God is lying to you. They may be misled by the degrees behind their name or by apparent previous pharmaceutical success, but the real Healer has been and will always be God. If a blind man could see that, then I pray you will also. Even in my spiritual dullness, I understood that reality.

The stories Sebi shared with me did not fit the biblical model. Even in my apostate condition, I expected certain "fruits," and the absence of those fueled my doubts about him and his methods. That was the Holy Spirit speaking to me. Would I listen? Based on what Sebi was telling me about himself, he had a keen interest in women. That is okay when in the context of marriage, otherwise it is sin. I could not shake the Holy Spirit's promptings, but there was Sebi's reputation to consider. After the session, Ronnie and the assistant came back to the room with the food, and I placed my conflicted feelings aside.

As I walked away with Ronnie, he and I discussed what Sebi's assistant had discussed with him while getting the food. I started.

"Sebi is a character."

"What do you mean?"

"Well, he told me about some of his travels and the people he's met. He loves his marijuana! He told me some stories about Mobile, my hometown, and some of the women he knew there. He's a very interesting guy."

Ronnie finished my thought. "Mananna is very protective of him, too. We talked about a lot of their travels too while we were getting lunch."

I wanted to say more but I didn't. Instead, I kept my misgivings to myself as Ronnie finished.

"Mananna and I hit it off well. I plan on staying in touch with her."

In fact, Ronnie would meet with them again and refer others to them. I held on to my reservations until I could resolve my conflicted feelings. Like all of us, Sebi was complicated, and although he had a reputation as a healer, he also had feet of clay. Ronnie and I laughed about it as we walked to the car.

My own experience confirmed my earlier misgivings. The herbal medicines Sebi had sold me raised my blood count to the highest level it had ever been. I was alarmed. Once I stopped taking the medicines, my blood count came back to its previous range. For me, that was the final confirmation. We are all given a measure of common sense and spiritual discernment. Working with Sebi taught me not to ignore either of those things.

Often, we ignore God's warning voice. In the moment, we trust what we see. What we don't see we don't trust, especially when it is inconvenient or goes against what we have been taught. I began to understand that ignoring God's warning voice is always a mistake. Sebi would be around in the area for some time, but I would not look at him the same way. My attitude had begun to change about "the Black cultural thing" too and the different aspects of it. Just because something is "Black" doesn't mean it is right or that it is good for you.

My confidence in well-meaning people had also been shaken. That had been true of White culture for some time, but now the same circumspection was being made necessary toward Black people and our cultural beliefs. The inconsistencies in life and morality, the diametrically opposing viewpoints, and a host of other things led me to question all I had learned. No, this was not the answer I was looking for. There was more. I knew that because I had experienced the "more" before.

Years later, I was told by a personal friend of Sebi that he had been heavily influenced by the Seventh-day Adventist health message. In fact, his grandmother had been an herbalist in her own right,[8] and his brother had been an Adventist minister. I have not been able to verify all of this information, nor disprove it, but I find it curious, nonetheless. Maybe my conflict about Sebi was the Spirit telling me what I was not ready to hear. As Jesus told Nicodemus, the wind blows where it will (see John 3:8). So it was with me.

Kamau Robinson

My friend, Kamau from the Kwame Nkrumah study group was sick but he was young and vibrant so I thought he would be fine. When I got the news about Kamau's death, it was only a day or so before his funeral and I was shocked and hurt. What happened, I wondered. He was a good person; life was so unfair. As I recall, Kamau's funeral was on a Thursday.

Before the burial, I had gotten a few more details about his short sickness and was told that his death was caused by some kind of virus or infection. It wasn't clear, and I was never satisfied with the explanation I was given, but dead is dead.

I was surprised when I arrived at the church in Northwest D.C. The fact that it was a Christian church was shocking. For as long as I had known Kamau, I could not recall him having anything positive to say about the Christian religion. On the contrary, his views were just the opposite. He felt that Christianity as he had experienced it was the cause of many of Black people's ills. The slave trade, the hypocrisy of chattel slavery, the lynchings of innocent Black men and women, Tulsa, and the Tuskegee experiments, and a world of hurt he all laid at the feet of Christian America. So, for him to have a Christian service was incongruous, to say the least.

The church was packed with proud Black men and women in their colorful kente and bogolanfini cloth attire. I wore mine proudly as well. The viewing line wrapped around the inside walls of the church all the way to the outside. Kamau had been loved in the community. I had come alone, but I did recognize some of the people there and saw a couple of people from the school and the study group. My mind kept drifting to why he was being funeralized in a church. As we paraded past the open casket, I just could not shake my questions. Would Kamau have approved of this? I knew the attitude of some of the people there about Christianity, and I knew that some of them would not set foot in a church unless it was for a funeral or a wedding. I wondered if African Americans would always be cultural orphans, estranged in a world of contradictions. Would we always have to search for our identity, with one foot in the motherland and the other on stolen soil?

Misgivings aside, I made my way to view Kamau's body. It all seemed so surreal. Kamau's whole life, what he stood for, what he believed, his personhood, his spirit, everything was gone. I thought about life, death, and what it all means. All the reasons I had stopped attending funerals came to my mind. I didn't like death, thinking about it, and especially being this close to it. As I stood in front of the casket, one thought kept ringing in my head. "Kamau, did you get it right?" "Kamau, did you get it right?" He had lived his life believing in a certain philosophy, a set of principles. Was it the right philosophy? Were they the right principles? Now, he would meet his Maker. The next voice he would hear would be that of his Creator God, his Judge. My Christian beliefs made me cringe for Kamau. I had this nagging sense that what the Bible said was true. I could not quote it exactly, but the theme was as clear as sunlight. It went something like this: the only name under heaven given among men whereby we must be saved was Jesus Christ (see Acts 4:12). I knew there was grace, but there was also choice.

I recalled all the things that Kamau and I used to talk about, like who built the pyramids or how many Africans were kidnapped and murdered in the European slave trade. How could we break the mental chains that so many Black people were still struggling with? How could we turn the tables and bring justice to this country? All of those questions and a thousand others seemed so relevant when we had discussed them. Now, as I stood at his coffin, they all faded into silence as had the memory of his voice. Only one thing remained: Eternity.

I was not there when Kamau died, so I truly cannot say if he got right with the God of the Bible. I had my doubts. One thing was certain, Kamau's chance was over, and that left me with another question: what about mine? The question rang in my mind again. Was I on the right path? Eternity was too important to be less than one hundred percent sure. I am certain that I had a puzzled look on my face as I paid my final respects.

The service proceeded like most other traditional Christian funerals. There was the music, the fond remembrances, and the eulogy. But there wasn't much discussion of heaven or hell. Those thoughts were on my mind, for sure. For the first time, I really had to give thought to what we, in the African Diaspora, believed. What was the consensus, the body of thinking, on life after death? And, most importantly, was it true? There were so many conflicting views that I had encountered in my recent experience, and none of them jived with my Christian upbringing. For certain, we had accepted an eclectic blend of theories, some very fanciful. There was the civilization of Kemet, which was eons old, and Atlantis, which was even more ancient. Some preached about reincarnation, astral bodies or higher plains of existence, alien seed races, and the list goes on. But as intriguing as they were, none rang true to me. This hodge-podge of ideas seemed more like potential scripts from *Star Trek* than a coherent plan laid out by a perfect Creator. It may have been my own predilection for simplicity, but none of what I had learned satisfied me as being valid.

That was a fact I could no longer ignore. From that point on, I began to search for real spiritual truth, spiritual certainty, all the while feeling that what I had previously abandoned was the very thing I was searching for. This was not a fork in the road but more of a slight right-angle turn in the direction I was already heading. Indeed, the integrative medical approach I had been following had exposed me to meditation, yoga, chakras, and chanting. I had even visited a Buddhist Temple. This path led me away from my Christian roots and into a world that I would find intriguing but antithetical to my upbringing. In my blindness, I had mistaken darkness for light and error for truth. The problem with deception is that the deceived don't know that they are deceived, and they will fight to remain that way.

The Color Purple

He was slightly younger than me with similar Southern roots, and he was a nice enough guy, but what I found strange about him was his penchant for the color purple. It was almost to the point of obsession. I could have probably called him Doctor Purple and he would not have been offended, but I never did. He was a transplant from New Orleans and had only recently moved to the D.C. area. Dr. P was trying very hard to make a name for himself as a holistic health practitioner in the Washington area. I had met him through one of my holistic doctors, Sullivan was her name, and when he left her to start a practice of his own, I followed. He bought a house on a busy street in Takoma Park and set up shop.

I was familiar with Takoma Park, since I had gone to college there. Takoma Park was a spiritual hub of sorts, with the presence of many new age religions. For many years, it had also been the center of the Seventh-day Adventist church. Its world headquarters, The General Conference of Seventh-day Adventists, had been located in the center of the town for almost seventy-five years. I felt that the juxtaposition of Adventism and all these new age religions was odd, until I recalled that God's people and message was always accompanied by the counterfeit in close proximity, as was the case with Moses' staff and Pharoah's magicians. The same was the case with Elijah and the priests of Baal with altars in close proximity.

As I mentioned, the good doctor's affinity for purple ran deep. All his clothes were the color violet as was his house. I learned that this was because of his religion, a form of Hinduism. The practice of yoga, meditation, and Kundalini were all key parts of his belief system. Supposedly, the crown chakra resonates a violet color and, according to Dr. P, it is the highest vibration, and thus his affinity. He was also vegan and ate mostly raw or slightly cooked foods. He made unusual combinations of food that were very tasty. Although he held private meditation sessions, I attended the group sessions held on Sunday mornings and Wednesday nights. Dr. P was also trained in acupuncture and had a section of the house dedicated to patients who came for treatment.

Most of his students were young, attractive, African American women. At the time, I did not think much about this, as I was focused on learning the disciplines he taught. Dr. P followed a guru who was well-known in New Orleans. I cannot recall the guru's name at present, but he was a small, pleasant man, quiet and laid back. He had an ashram in the west—I believe it was in Arizona. He came to visit once while I was studying with Dr. P, and I met him and had an audience with him.

We met in a sparsely furnished and dimly lit room in the attic portion of the house. I did most of the talking. Every so often, he would interject words of wisdom, but he was mostly silent. I never really felt comfortable throughout the session, but I thought I was being enlightened, so I continued anyway. If you have seen the movie *The Razor's Edge* with Tyrone Power or the remake with Bill Murray, that is what it felt like to me. The only thing absent was the Himalayan Mountains. As I reflect, it all seems so melodramatic, but at the time, it was serious business. The guru lived an ascetic life—strictly vegan, daily hours of meditation, and very few creature comforts. He was the polar opposite of Sebi and more of what I thought a "holy man" should be like. However, there was still something missing. This experience was different than anything I had encountered so far, but there were some core similarities.

My new guru and Dr. P recommended a complete list of reading materials, all of which I would eventually discard or burn. Many of them dealt with mediation, but some included the writings of Madame Blavatsky and Albert Pike. And yes, the binder they came in was purple. I ordered many of the books. These books taught a secret knowledge, and I found many of them fascinating. They explained spiritual things from a very different perspective. All life was spiritual. The universe was one, and it was spiritual. God was everything and in everything. If this sounds like pantheism, that is because it is. The secret knowledge of good and evil was the same promise that was held out to Adam and Eve in the Garden of Eden. Had they known the true face of evil, they would have turned away immediately. I also would have turned away. This secret knowledge ran the gamut of secret societies such as the Masons, Templars, Rosicrucians, and others. But one author stood out to me; her name was Helena Blavatsky.

Helena was born in 1831 and was contemporaneous with a woman whose writings I was familiar with; Ellen G. White. What Blavatsky taught was diametrically opposed to the beliefs of Mrs. White, and though at that time I had issue with some of Mrs. White's writings, I felt uncomfortable with the secret knowledge that was being presented to me. Notice again, wherever God places His alter, Satan places one nearby. At first it seemed dark to me, yet I continued down the forbidden path. I trusted Dr. P and his mentor. There was that "voice" again, but by this time I could barely recognize it.

This so-called secret knowledge crossed centuries, nations, and all ethnic barriers. Most importantly, it was supernatural and emphasized a power from within which I had direct access to and could manipulate. This supernatural element was the real cement that glued all these beliefs together. The good and the evil were right in front of me, and yet I could not distinguish the difference between them.

These beliefs were not just diametrically opposed to Christian teaching, they had an animosity toward it. In some instances, they even took Christian symbols and distorted or profaned them. An example is the upside-down cross which many Satanists wear as a sign of devotion. This hatred was consistent across all the books I read. In some instances, it was more subtle, but it was always there. The hatred was consistent and very purposeful. That should have been a clue to the real agenda of the secret societies. I knew enough to know that it was not just my perspective. Having shared that animosity with others myself, I knew it was real. With all I had seen and learned, I kept moving forward into the darkness. Step by step and little by little, I was being led further and further to the point of no return. It seemed that with all my gaining of knowledge, my center of critical thinking had been shut off, especially to what I had learned and believed most of my life.

Pan-Africanist ideals and new age religions had many things in common, like positive vibes and healthy eating. I had met some wonderful people with good intentions, but at the end of the day none of that really mattered. I had to get it right for myself. Seeing Kamau in a pine box had taught me that. Yes, I had to know the truth because only the truth would set me free, and that was not a cliché. Was heaven real? Was the God of the Bible the one true God? Who had it right? These were questions bigger than my mortgage note.

I probably studied with Dr. P for nearly two years, and his classes began to fill up. I had gotten to know some of the regular attendees. In particular, I knew one because she was also a real estate investor. I saw her at a shop in Baltimore, and we had lunch. We both owned property in Baltimore at that time and exchanged notes on our experiences. We chatted for a good bit, but the exchange I remember most involved Dr. P.

"What made you start investing in Baltimore?" I asked.

"Well houses are cheaper here and there's an abundance of renters. It was a good mix and a good place to get started."

"Same here, but Baltimore is too easy on renters and too hard on landlords," I countered.

She continued, "Investing in Baltimore is not for the faint of heart that's for sure." There was a pause in our conversation as she took a sip of coffee. I began again.

"I haven't seen you at the sessions for a while. You've been busy with real estate?"

Her reply was quick and to the point, almost like she was waiting for the question.

"No, I stopped coming because I was angry and hurt. Dr. P (she didn't call him that) was full of himself and he lied to me."

I was speechless and not prepared for where our conversation was heading. With cold emotion she continued. "We were in a romantic relationship for a good while, when I found out that he was having other relationships with other women in the sessions. That hurt me, but what hurt the most is that he married a young White girl with nothing to offer him. I'm a Black professional woman; we all were Black professional women, and he married a young White girl with nothing."

Thankfully, she didn't say anymore. In my shock and chagrin, I muttered, "Wow, man, I didn't know that. I wondered why the groups had gotten smaller."

I had met his wife and she was indeed young, White, and demure. She wore purple sarongs with contrasting purple hijabs. Her modest attire complimented her average looks. She and Dr. P had very different personalities and I wondered how they got together, but I didn't tell my lunch-mate that. Until that time, I had no idea about their relationship or the underpinning drama. Even then, it was really none of my business. Silently, I tried to reconcile my emotions.

Dr. P was a young, handsome, Black man, but I had never really thought of him as anything other than a "holy man." His ascetic lifestyle seemed out of place with what I'd just been told. I viewed him as a teacher and an example. I was disappointed by his alleged philandering, and the race thing she tied into it only exacerbated the hurt. Of course, a woman scorned is no small thing, and it made sense as to why she would mention it to me. It had the intended effect.

As I walked back to my car, I shook my head both literally and figuratively. What she shared had changed my thinking on what I had learned of his philosophy and how I felt about Doctor P. I also remembered my experience with Sebi and my similar disappointment with him. What was I doing? I had gone down too many blind alleys. Was it me? No, I expected a higher moral standard. I needed something I could believe in, someone I could trust with my life, something that was just not available in all these new age philosophies I had been pursuing. I could not build a foundation for eternity on sand; it had to be built on solid rock. That was the only foundation that made sense. The feeling would not go away.

In retrospect, it is clear. The beliefs that these men shared were similar. Their highest standard was a human standard. They considered themselves good men, but in the end, they were still men. I could not ride their coattails to heaven, but hell was another matter. I had to make my own decisions. Doctor P believed in reincarnation, also called metempsychosis. Reincarnation professes to allow the soul to grow into perfection over a series of lifetimes. So, if you don't get it right in this lifetime, you will have another chance. The doctrine of karma is the essence of this belief. Christians know it as salvation by works. If you are a good person at heart and you live to help others, the sentiment goes, then God will bless you, and you are guaranteed a ticket to heaven. I did not find a lot of comfort in that belief. One lifetime is enough, especially if it is full of pain and heartache. Doctor P was wrong—I knew it. But I felt stuck with no way out.

This latest disappointment cast a pall of doubt over the direction I was heading. Once the enemy grabs a hold of you, he does his best to keep you ensnared. I was experiencing an unsavory mix of emotions. My business was okay, and I felt poised to go to the next level with national exposure, but I had hit a glass ceiling. I had ambitions of becoming the first true African American real estate investment guru, with the likes of Robert Kiyosaki. I personally knew one of the men Kiyosaki had consulted with prior to his book launch. This man thought that what I was doing was just as good as some of Kiyosaki's ideas, but no matter how hard I tried, I could not get to the next level. On four different occasions, I had the opportunity to purchase office buildings, but each deal fell apart. I could not explain it, and it made no sense. I had misplaced priorities, which caused the rest of my life to be unsettled. I wasn't spending enough time with my family, and I was working all the time and I was not happy.

Later, my wife told me that during that time of our lives, she was the closest she had ever been to God. She prayed for me constantly. I now realize that her prayers were the covering that kept me from eternal ruin. I do not say this lightly either. Sometime later, she told me what had happened. I share it with you in the hope that you will learn from her experience. One morning, while she was praying earnestly and asking God to save me, she heard the Holy Spirit as clearly as a church bell on Sunday morning. He said, "Don't pray that prayer again. I have heard your prayer." Cassandra was shocked. She had prayed that prayer for thirteen years! God answered her in a way she never expected.

When I share what her prayers did, it brings chills to my body. One day, as I was in my yoga posture, chanting and meditating, I began to feel strange. Suddenly, it felt like my body was flying, and I was traveling in space. I could see stars and galaxies close up. I seemed to be beyond time and space. What I was feeling was called astral travel, or an out-of-body experience. It was unbelievable and I could not explain it. I had read about other people having similar experiences, but when it happened to me, I was both frightened and excited at the same time. This event was clearly supernatural. What was next? I was not sure, but I couldn't stop. I wanted more. That was the enemy raising the stakes, giving me a taste of the power of the occult.

At the time, what I did not realize was that my wife's prayers established the boundary over which the enemy could not step, both in the spiritual and in the physical worlds. The Holy Spirit would stop what I could not stop. Now I understand. My eternal soul was on the line. God knew how close I was to eternal ruin. I had no clue. The lesson is simple: husbands pray for your wives, wives pray for your husbands, parents pray for your children, church members pray for each other. Pray without ceasing. Pray until God tells you to stop. He will answer your prayers. He has promised to do so. God's Word tells us, "The earnest prayer of a righteous person has great power and produces wonderful results" (see James 5:16). So often I had taken prayer for granted, and that was a mistake. Jesus shared a parable with His disciples and with us:

> And he spake a parable unto them to this end, that men ought always to pray, and not to faint; Saying, There was in a city a judge, which feared not God, neither regarded man: And there was a widow in that city; and she came unto him, saying, Avenge me of mine adversary. And he would not for a while: but afterward he said within himself, Though I fear not God, nor regard man; Yet because this widow troubleth me, I will avenge her, lest by her continual coming she weary me. And the Lord said, Hear what the unjust judge saith. And shall not God avenge his own elect, which cry day and night unto him, though he bear long with them? I tell you that he will avenge them speedily. Nevertheless when the Son of man cometh, shall he find faith on the earth?
>
> —*Luke 18:1-8 KJV*

My wife prayed for 13 years. The Lord heard every prayer she uttered, and He was orchestrating affairs in my life all the while. He did not delay—His timing was perfect. As I look back, I can see why certain things happened for me and why others did not. My plans might have made me rich and famous, but at an eternal cost, and not just for me, but for those around me. How can one measure the influence, for good or for evil, that we have on our immediate family and friends? Only God can.

CHAPTER 7

Turning Third, Sliding Into Home

My *search for truth led me down* many fruitless paths, and one of those paths had a unique signpost, a book entitled *Metu Neter.* It was essentially Egyptian theology with some modern adaptations, which included yoga and meditation. Ra Un Nefer Amen is the book's author, and he has a very interesting background. He had a large following in New York City and was considered a spiritual leader. I had the book for years sitting on my shelf but had never read it. Then one day, I picked it up and was intrigued by much of what it discussed. For sure, much of the teaching was information I had become acquainted with, but the Afrocentric message was right in line with what I had been studying. It was also an instruction manual on the various practices of the religion. Basically, the author laid out a step-by-step guide to its spiritual practice. Central to the practice was divination with the use of oracles similar to tarot cards.

Using the techniques outlined, one could supposedly summon ancestors and Egyptian gods for help in daily life situations. This too was nothing but spiritualism. Let's be clear; I was still involved in other new age disciplines as I studied Metu Neter, but they did not contradict each other. In fact, they buttressed one another. This reinforcement of ideas had a compounding effect, similar to the belief that the more you hear the same thing, the truer it must be. Culture and entertainment also played into this dynamic. Ideas like evolution and the immortality of the soul saturate movies and television. This noise drowns out that still, small voice of Truth.

As I delved deeper into the book, I soon realized that there was something really different about it. The things I read were just too insightful to come from one person alone. I began to suspect that it was supernatural, which was both frightening and appealing. I was on very dangerous ground, yet I thought I was being enlightened. The book introduced me to Egyptian deities, some of which the Bible talks about. At the time, though, I did not realize that. Since the beginning of time, the enemy has used these same tricks. Why? Because they work.

The way the author wove meditation, African culture, and ancient rites into a cohesive body and daily practice was the reason I think it was so appealing to me. I didn't just read the book, I studied it. It referenced other materials to support its version of the truth, and I looked into those as well. One thing that kept me from falling completely in line was how the book discussed God. It said that God was unable to experience what we humans must endure, and this limitation is why He needed us. For me, that stuck out like a sore thumb. If God is omniscient, omnipresent, and omnipotent, why would He not be able to experience what we do? Then there was Christ. Didn't Christ suffer as we suffer? Was His life a lie? That was a contradiction to me, and I could not be fully engaged in this theory because of it.

My loving wife was very patient with me as I went down the wide and dangerous path at full throttle. We were approaching 2008, and we were in an election cycle. The real estate market was booming, and I did not see the end coming. If I did, I ignored it. There were signs, but greed has a way of blinding people to the obvious. Then it all began to unravel. The market tanked, and the real estate bubble went "pop." With it, so did my real estate brokerage. We thought the downturn wouldn't last for long, but we were wrong in both the length and the severity of it. Whereas before the Great Recession, you could do a bad deal and still make money, that was no longer the case. There were no deals to be had, good or bad. The way everyone had been doing business was over. It was like the old, wild, and lawless west when a new sheriff came to town.

Mortgage brokers and real estate agents began to panic. Banks' funds dried up, and no one was lending. Foreclosures went through the roof, and Fortune 500 companies were dropping like flies. Wall Street staples, with household names like Lehman Brothers and AIG, had to have government bailouts. Investors who I knew, with dozens of houses, lost everything. I knew people that committed suicide during the downturn. Sabrina, who I sublet office space to, had a net-branch mortgage brokerage. She owned quite a few investment properties, and as her tenants became delinquent, so did she. One by one, she lost each house until finally she lost the one that she and her five children lived in. Her brokerage closed, and she went to work as a processor, managing foreclosures for a servicer. Hers was not an isolated case. I knew married couples with once-thriving businesses, who hid out in their parents' basements to avoid debt collectors and disgruntled investors looking for them. Although it was a bad time for agents, I believe it was even worse for mortgage brokers. I think only one in fifty survived, literally.

I had saved some money, but not nearly enough to ride out the downturn. The timing was perfect. As the bills kept coming in and the money kept going out, God got my attention. I had recently finished building my dream home on the water, and now I watched the market value of my house drop precipitously. The problem was that my mortgage payment stayed the same. Soon, the whole neighborhood was upside down as far as property values went, and foreclosure notices began to pop up like popcorn. In fact, of the 38 properties in my neighborhood, 24 would ultimately end up in foreclosure. Indeed, it was the worst of times for the real estate industry. My business was no exception. At one point, I had employed nearly 40 agents and support staff, but that number dwindled down to three. My only option was business bankruptcy, and that was a very difficult pill to swallow.

I hired a bankruptcy attorney from Rockville, and she was very proficient in what she did. Mentally, though the process was very difficult for me to manage. It was so impersonal, yet I took it personally. My business was an extension of my personality and when it failed, I failed. My ego was crushed. It didn't help that my bankruptcy trustee did not seem to like me. Then again, that could have been my perception. She was only doing her job. At any rate, I got a storage unit and moved most of my office furnishings into it. I had every intention of starting up again once the market came back. My plan was optimistic and I was naïve. That is a dangerous combination. A year turned into two, then three, and would ultimately stretch to seven years. In my general area, markets would get better. But Prince George's County, where I lived, lagged behind. In fact, as I write this, property values are still less than half of what they were in 2008.

The prospect of losing everything I had worked for heightened my interest in religion and in getting right with God. In fact, that was the case with many of the people in the real estate business. Of course, there were others who tried to get on with life as usual, but it was anything but business as usual. By 2009, my income had shrunk to 1 percent of what it had been in 2007. Yes, that is correct—1 percent!

Like many others in similar situations, I was desperate. My children were in private school. I had a ridiculous mortgage note and very little income. I needed help. I began to go to my wife's church, as well as continuing with my other religious activities. Then Dr. P called, even though I hadn't met with him for a while. He told me of a man from California who was well-known in spiritual circles. This man would be doing a "flower reading." Now, I truly didn't know what a flower reading was, but because I was curious and needed some direction, I went.

A flower reading was really a psychic reading. I told my close friend, Ronnie, who previously had gone to Sebi's with me, and we went together. The reading was held in a nice apartment complex on Connecticut Avenue in Northwest D.C. There was a nicely appointed auditorium in the building, and about ten people attended. As I recall, most were white with about three African Americans. The psychic took his time with each of us. He did a general reading for each one of us in attendance. Many of the things he said about me were right on point. I was surprised at how much he knew about me, and I signed up for the private reading. At first, I thought it was the power of suggestion, but after really thinking about what he had said about me, I knew better.

In the private session, he used a tape recorder to tape the reading. The session was about fifty minutes long, and the recording was given to me when I left. Much of what he told me about myself was true. It was uncanny. I listened to that tape repeatedly, as he explained my chakras, their colors, and what they meant. I was so deep into the occult that it would take a miracle to get me out. I truly didn't know what else to do. There was no way out on my own.

Ascent From Darkness

Then came Peter to Him, and said, Lord, how oft [often] shall my brother sin against me, and I forgive him? till seven times? Jesus saith unto him, I say not unto thee, Until seven times; but, Until seventy times seven.

—*Matthew 18:21 KJV*

I was drowning financially. I was confused about the direction of my life and I didn't know where to turn for help. I was at wit's end. "Oh, but God!" I began to pray and ask God for guidance. I was desperate. Then Ronnie, who I had gone to the flower reading with, called and told me there was going to be a similar event at the Metu Neter center in D.C. "How lucky," I thought to myself. I told him I would go with him, but the event was on a Saturday, which was the same day my wife went to church.

As the day approached, I was committed to going to the reading, but I also had a strong impression that I should not go. I couldn't make up my mind. Finally, the day of the reading, I decided I would go. I felt very uncomfortable about my decision but really didn't know why. As I recall, I was dressed for the occasion, but I just could not go. Instead, I was impressed to go to Capitol Hill Seventh-day Adventist Church. As I sat in the pew listening to Pastor Gene Donaldson, his message struck a chord in me. It was as if he was speaking directly to me. I did think about what was going on at the other center, but I knew I had made the right choice. Pastor Donaldson preached on the story of the twelve men who were sent to spy out the Promised Land for the Children of Israel.

Of the twelve men sent out, only two felt confident that, with the help of God, they could take the land. They were in the minority, and the ten others won the day. This was in spite all of them having witnessed the miracles that God had done for the people of Israel while they were in the land of Egypt. I recalled some of the miracles God had done in my life. As the sermon was closing, the pastor made a two-part altar call. The first one was the "simply stand to your feet if you want to change your life" call. I stood along with many others in the congregation. That wasn't so hard. I needed to change my life. However, the second appeal was for those who wanted to give their life to Jesus, to come to the front. Now, that was where I drew the line. My mind had been filled with years of falsehoods, one brick laid on top of the other, lie upon lie. This had gone on for so long that the simple, plain truth seemed too simple, too plain. Life was much more complicated than a yes or no.

With my eyes closed tightly, I started talking to God right then and there. It was really more like venting than talking. How could all of the things I had learned be wrong? Christianity seemed mundane by comparison. God creating the world in six days—that was impossible! I knew better. My thoughts raced back and forth. Finally, in desperation I asked God, "If You really want me to do this, You will have to let me know in a real, tangible way." I did not expect anything to happen, but no sooner had the thought left my mind when someone tapped me on the shoulder. It wasn't a light tap either. The jolt made me open my eyes, but to my surprise, there was no one there. No one was even close to me. A church elder, Michael Cox stood toward the back of the church in the mid-aisle. His eyes met mine and we both seemed surprised. He had not touched me, as he was too far away. I knew that this was the indisputable sign I had asked for. God had literally touched me! I could not contain my emotions. I moved toward the pastor with tears streaming down my face, crying like a baby. Soon my wife joined me, and so did other family members and friends. We all cried together. God had brought me back. God had brought me home. Cassandra had prayed for thirteen years, and God performed a miracle. I stood there surrounded by family and friends, and one Scripture kept going through my mind. I am not sure how it got there, but I kept repeating it. It was Philippians 4:13: "I can do all things through Christ who strengthens me" (NKJV).

I had no second thoughts—I knew I had made the right decision. My struggle was far from over, and in many ways, it had just begun. But that Scripture was all the promise I needed. I began to read my Bible and pray daily. I became a staple in Sabbath School, so much so that the superintendent asked me to teach. I thought Lori Mathis was joking at first, but she was very serious. That would be followed by participation in prison ministry, then feeding the homeless. The church leadership asked me to be a deacon. I was more than happy to help. I had a lot of lost time to make up for.

The Holy Spirit also had some work for me to do. I had been deeply entrenched in the occult world, and the enemy had access to my body and mind. But you can only serve one master. I had made my choice, and the Holy Spirit impressed me to do some very specific things. I was impressed to throw away or burn all the books that I had collected so meticulously. Most of them were in my library, across from our bedroom, and there were lots of them.

I remember gathering an arm full of books and driving them to the park near my house to burn them. The park had stationary grills that were far away from anything that could catch fire. As I came down the steps, I glanced over my shoulder to see a large shadow, and I felt an unholy presence, which scared me to the point that I started to run. It was real, it was frightening, and I knew it was the enemy. Later, I also found a ten-gallon metal drum and used it to burn more of the occult books, one by one. I would not turn back. I was convicted, and I knew my God was able to protect me.

It disturbed me to think that I had invited demons into my house and to where my family lived. I burned, destroyed, and got rid of every single book that even remotely had to do with new age religions and secret societies, anything occult. That included *Metu Neter* and the oracle cards that came with it. I had actually hidden the cards, but to my surprise, my wife had already come across the cards and had thrown them out. She told me that the Holy Spirit had led her to them. I was not surprised. It was confirmation of my decision, and I was grateful to her. I also got rid of paintings and sculptures that were questionable.

The enemy had planted lies in my mind—one in particular. The yin-yang philosophy posits that there is a duality in the universe: the concept of equal yet opposite forces that are complimentary, good and evil. It says that one cannot exist without the other. It says that God is impersonal. The universe is a principle— a cosmic mind. All of those things are lies. I had to learn the truth. It was like learning to walk again. God is good. Satan is evil. God is omnipotent. Satan is impotent by comparison. God is eternal. Satan will perish. God made man in His image. Satan desires to remake man in his image. For so many years, I had believed the lies and the other falsehoods that they had spawned. It would take time to change those wrong habits of thinking.

Around that time, I became familiar with an author named Roger Morneau, who had written several books on prayer. He had an incredible story with some similar aspects as mine. I found his books invaluable as I started down the path to freedom from the occult. I will discuss Morneau in more detail later. The enemy would not let me go without a fight, but I had the Bible and Philippians 4:13. Morneau's books and videos, which were on YouTube, helped me to understand some of the strategies of the enemy and how serious I must be in my walk with the Lord. I moved forward in faith.

My financial situation did not improve right away, but God made a way for my family. I was behind on the mortgage note and hardly making any money, but still He provided. I, of course, was paying a loyal tithe with what little money I had. It was a struggle but God works in amazing ways.

My wife and I were home one summer evening when storm clouds began to quickly gather. We were in the house, and our main concern was that the wind, which was blowing hard, would topple a tree onto the house. Suddenly, we heard a loud thunderclap and a brilliant flash of pink light right outside our kitchen window. It was so loud and bright it scared us nearly half to death. The lights in the house went out as we tried to gather our wits. Lightening had struck the house! Realizing what had happened, we looked outside the window to see what damage had been done. It was substantial. The rear deck had burn marks, and some of the flooring was missing. Several electrical sockets were out, as were our computers. Even our sewage grinder was blown and some of the caps on our deck railing were missing. Still, it could have been worse. The lightning hit only inches away from a container of lighter fluid we used for our outdoor grill. If it had hit that fluid container, there would have been an explosion and a fire. God prevailed.

The insurance claim we filed not only allowed us to get the exterior deck fixed but also to get the sewage grinder repaired. There was also another miracle that helped us through. I was going over a bank statement I had and saw that there was a balance of $6,700. There is only one explanation for how that money got there because I never made that deposit. There were so many incidents like that—it was amazing!

With the failure and bankruptcy of my business came the inevitable delinquency of my mortgage note. I had some money saved, but my mortgage payment was over $12,000 per month. It is amazing how quickly I went through my savings trying to stay current. Although those were stressful and dire times, God used them to mold me and build my faith, as the potter molds the clay. I was worried about my house being foreclosed, and I was also concerned about the real estate climate. Maybe I was paranoid, but the newspapers were full of real estate schemes and outright fraud.

People I knew in real estate were losing their businesses and houses. Some of them were desperate. Stress can make a person do all kinds of things. I myself was looking for a lifeline and began to grasp for straws. Around that time, an investor friend introduced me to a couple who, he said, were great at locating deals. They were a Black couple. I should have asked him the question, "Why aren't they giving you the deals?" but I didn't. We all met and hit it off. We agreed to work together. The market was rough and money was tight, and I was still doing business the only way I knew how. It wasn't working.

The couple was true to their word and brought me deal after deal, but there always seemed to be a catch to each one. With all my experience and know-how, I should have been able to make progress, but every real estate deal that I tried to complete, simply failed. Deals that I should have been able to do in my sleep wouldn't close. Deals just fell apart for no reason. I couldn't understand it. It was like a curse was on me.

At that time, the news was full of reports of mortgage scams and lenders going to jail, and Prince George's County had several high-profile residents who would end up in prison. I knew several of them, by reputation, who had to serve time, although I had never worked directly with them. Loan officers, appraisers, and some title attorneys were all under suspicion and were easy targets. I was a real estate broker and not involved in the lending process, so that shielded me somewhat, but it didn't exempt me. The powers that be needed to blame somebody for the financial debacle, and they went after the low-hanging fruit. If you had made money in the business, you were automatically suspect, and I had made money and, in the process, some enemies.

Two mortgage brokers that I knew of, but never worked with, made headlines in the *Washington Post*. One had had a fabulous $800,000 wedding where Patti Labelle sang.[9] The female broker was a principal in the Metropolitan Money Store and was convicted of defrauding homeowners out of

$37 million. She was eventually sentenced to 12 years in prison. An FBI informant was planted inside the mortgage business of the other broker; Charles was his name. Both brokers ended up in prison. Charles was convicted of defrauding the public of nearly $25 million. There were many others, both small and large, taking advantage of the system and of people who looked like them. Greed is truly color-blind.

Even people who had only cut corners but had not done anything illegal were paranoid. Guilt by association was the fear a lot of people in the business had. The government could require that mortgage brokers turn over files as old as 10 years. They could then review all the paperwork related to a specific loan and require the broker to buy the loan back if anything was found inappropriate in the file. That drove most of the remaining larger firms out of the business. Later, I would come to see this as part of a larger government scheme.

Appraisers were accused of inflating values, and a couple of them whom I knew also ended up in jail. I was an appraiser too and had employed other appraisers. I made it a point to look over my files for any irregularities. I was also investing and had a concern about several cases on our books. I would eventually let my appraisal license lapse so as not to create a conflict with my brokerage business. Still, I had an uneasy feeling that I just could not get rid of. I was worrying a lot and praying even more.

Then one night I had a very vivid dream. In the dream, I looked out the window of my bedroom, and I saw a couple who were dressed in black. They were standing on the grass in my front yard, looking at my house. In the dream, I was impressed that they could not harm me but that they were watching me. I was also impressed that they worked for the government. One was a man, and the other a woman. The dream unnerved me, and if I had been paranoid before, I was now on the verge of panic.

The next day, I made it a point to pray as David had in Psalm 51. I asked God to forgive me and to create in me a clean heart. I fell on my knees and pleaded with the Almighty. I felt my unworthiness. I felt my great need, and I knew that with all I had done, only God could forgive me. As I finished praying with tears of genuine remorse, I stayed on my knees and gazed up toward the bedroom window. There was a stream of sunlight beaming through. With it came a sense of peace and calm that I had only experienced once before, when I was a young man and God had spoken to me and delivered me from a self-inflicted disaster. At that instant, I knew that I had been forgiven. I praised Him!

It is important that I note a contrast here. When I previously had an out-of-body experience, it was electric and sense oriented. It was designed to intoxicate me and make me spellbound with awe, like a movie that has music, special effects, and theatrics. That is how the devil works. He appeals to the senses, at the expense of reason, and it is very effective. This doesn't just work in movies, concerts, and Super Bowls. We see this very often in many churches too. The pulsating music, the speaker and singer's voices cascading higher and louder, and the audience praising at the top of their lungs, often in tongues, combine to overwhelm the senses and negate reason. But in this latest incident of my life, that was not the case. God does not rely on theatrics and special effects. He doesn't have to. He appeals to reason. He said so in His word:

> Come now, and let us reason together, saith the Lord: though your sins be as scarlet, they shall be as white as snow; though they be red like crimson, they shall be as wool.
>
> —*Isaiah 1:18 KJV*

God has given man the ability to choose. Choice based on coercion and over-wrought emotions is not God's design. He invites us to reason with Him, to taste and see His goodness. He simply wills something to happen and it is so. The calm I felt was both rational and emotional, but it was emotion subject to reason. It was genuine. The sense of peace I felt was genuine too. I remained calm while nothing in my world had visibly changed.

A day or so later, I met with my investor friend and his two associates at my house. I had an idea for getting some business by using social media, and I pulled out my video camera to take a video of everyone. The husband abruptly got up out of his seat and said I could not take a picture of him. He was adamant and would not give a reason as to why. I was startled and perplexed by his attitude, but I didn't press the matter. Now, my dream was beginning to make perfect sense. Were these the two people I had seen standing on my lawn observing me? Had God been protecting me all along and that is why we never could get a deal closed when they were involved? I would never know for sure, but I was strongly convicted that this was indeed the case. I made up my mind then and there that I would not work with them in the future, even though I didn't tell them right then. I also had some doubts about the investor friend who made the initial introduction. Why hadn't they given the so-called deals to my investor friend instead of me? What did he know? Was I being set up? Was my friend being duped too? I would never know for sure, but I had my warning, and I would heed it.

The mortgage foreclosure tsunami was in the headlines daily. The stories about lender fraud and subprime loans got the attention of legislators and created a cottage industry of lawyers fighting the abuses that had been uncovered. "Show me the note," became a legitimate defense of many people losing their homes, and that cry could be heard all around the country. I had a subprime loan, and my lender was GMAC Mortgage, which was one of the most egregious abusers. Once I got behind in my mortgage payments, I knew it would be impossible for me to get caught up. Foreclosure was inevitable.

I became desperate for that grand-slam deal, but nothing was happening. Along with my wife, I began to pray, as we feared the worst. My brother and his family were having financial difficulties and moved in with us. They would end up staying with us for nearly five years. If we lost our house, two families would be displaced. I was hemmed in on all sides with the Red Sea ahead and the mortgage company, like Pharaoh's army, in hot pursuit. I had to break the news to my daughters and the rest of the family, but I needed the right moment.

My brother-in-law, Terrell, was the chef at a restaurant in D.C. As our family gathered for a Sunday brunch, my wife, daughters, and myself were all seated together in a booth. The rest of our family was there as well, but at separate tables. My mood was gloomy, and I could see that my daughters knew something was wrong. With all my years of experience in real estate, with all my expertise as an investor, with all my vaunted resourcefulness, I felt completely helpless. With humility, I explained to my children the situation. My youngest daughter, Xavian, began to cry profusely, as she looked at me expecting a solution. Her tears exaggerated my feelings of helplessness. I started crying too, and soon people in the restaurant began to notice. I mustered all the pride I had and pulled myself together, letting my family know that this was not the end. God was in charge, but my nascent faith had not been tested under circumstances like this before.

Shortly after that, while working at home, I was walking from my office to the kitchen when I saw a notice posted on the front door. I became physically sick and grabbed my stomach so I wouldn't throw-up. It was as I feared, a Notice of Default. GMAC was going to foreclose, and we had about 45 days to prevent it. Lord, help me. Praying and reading the Bible at least two hours a day became part of my morning routine. Of course, I had to tell my brother and his wife. I also told my mother. Each one of us was praying.

Shortly thereafter, I got a call from one of the elders at Capitol Hill Church, Saundra Austin. She very abruptly announced that the Lord had told her to come over and anoint my house. Now, I did not know Saundra well, but she pressed the issue, and I wasn't one to turn down prayer, especially in my circumstance. At that time, she lived in Fort Washington and was at my house in about half an hour. She parked on my street and, with anointing oil in hand, asked me to show her the outline of the whole lot. I looked at her as a deer does when paralyzed in the headlights of a fast-approaching car. With anointing oil in hand, she started praying as if she meant it. As she went, she gave me instructions. "This is how you do it," she said. We started at the house and anointed every door and corner. We then walked over the entire lot, with Saundra praying and me tagging along. That was on a Thursday morning. After we had finished, I waved goodbye and stood there for a moment wondering about these strange happenings.

GMAC tried to foreclose on us for nearly six years. This was truly a trial of fire and a walk of faith. We did a loan modification. I ended up hiring six separate groups of attorneys or foreclosure consultants. In that same period, we received three separate notices of defaults, but every time they tried to foreclose, the Lord would intervene in a miraculous way. Every time. I don't believe I ever missed a Thursday of anointing my house in all that time. Then the fateful time arrived. We received the Prince George's County paperwork to go to mediation with GMAC. I'd had many sleepless nights over the period of our struggle with the bank, but the week leading up to the mediation was truly trying.

We had an attorney, but we knew that the odds were not in our favor. It would take a miracle, a substantial miracle, to save our house. We were delinquent for over $500,000! Even worse, market values in our neighborhood were only about a third of what they had been when we first built our house. Yes, things looked bleak. Oh, but God! The week of the mediation, which was on a Friday morning, I fasted and prayed. I asked my wife to fast with me, and she did.

That Thursday, as I started out to anoint the house and the land, the Holy Spirit spoke to me. My routine had been to start on the left side of the house with my back to the front door, but that Thursday was different. The Holy Spirit told me to walk around my house seven times, starting from the right, my back to the front door. I was puzzled, and I was not certain if God was really speaking to me. The enemy was filling my head with doubt, but I was obedient. I walked around the house six times, and the seventh time I anointed it as I walked. Had God really spoken to me? I would have my answer the very next day. The outcome of the mediation was in God's hands, as it had always been. Seven times around my house were my walls of Jericho experience.

My wife took off from school that Friday, and we drove to the courthouse in Upper Marlboro. It was a bright, sunny, autumn day. We were both nervous as we got directions to the building where the mediation would be held. We were there early and took our seats in the judge's chambers. We exchanged pleasantries with the judge, and he casually explained to us the process. He let us know that he was retired and that the state had only started the mediation process for homeowners after the public outcry over bank abuses. They had to do something to help people in our situation, if only for the aesthetics. He further explained that he had no real power to make the bank do anything, but we would at least be able to air our grievances. By then, I was thinking that the whole system was a farce. Our spirits sank as our attorney came into the room.

While we were waiting on the bank's attorney to arrive, we went outside to speak with our attorney, Brian. As we talked, Brian told us what we should expect and that, at best, we could try to get the bank to give us time to move, even though it had already been over five years. We didn't hold out much hope. Brian shrugged his shoulders as the bank's female attorney turned the corner, a bit flustered for being late. She greeted us and we all went into the court chambers together. We took our respective places, and the judge went through his protocol.

The attorney, a young, White woman, was fresh out of law school, and this was her very first case. She had only arrived in town that very morning and hadn't even unpacked her suitcase yet. None of this seemed to bode well for our cause. It all seemed so perfunctory. I was silently praying as she finished her introduction—then the judge took over. He pulled the speakerphone closer to himself and explained that he had been instructed to call the bank's senior attorney—she too was female. He did so as we nervously waited. She was somewhere in the Midwest. She answered the phone and introduced herself to us and to the junior attorney we had just met. She was very pleasant—you might even say bubbly. I thought her attitude was a façade, and that upset me even more.

After our brief pleasantries, her attention turned to the matter at hand. She began. "You guys have a beautiful home. The appraiser's photos don't do it justice." We didn't know what to say. I wondered if this was what executioners did before they pulled the switch. She continued. "Let me say first, we don't want to take your home." Again, we remained silent, waiting for the next shoe to drop. She then asked, "Mr. Arnold, you're a realtor. How much is your home worth?" I had prepared for that question, and I looked at Brian. Brian spoke for me. "Based on what we could come up with, considering current market conditions, maybe $1.1 million." We knew that number was high, but I also knew that the bank wouldn't entertain anything lower than that. She quickly retorted, "No, I don't think so." *"Here we go,"* I thought.

Brian hesitantly responded as he looked at me. "Can you give us a minute?" She agreed, and Brian and I stepped outside. Our conversation was brief and uncertain. I couldn't pay for the house even at $1.1 million. If they wanted more, it would kill all hope of us making a deal. We discussed my options and came to the same conclusion. I had none. We went back inside at the mercy of the bank, but in the grace of God. With little conviction, we reduced our number. She picked up where she left off. "I think your house is worth about $315,000." In that instant, I fell back in my chair, looked at my wife, and thought, "Just look at God!" The Red Sea had just parted, and we were about to walk through on dry land. What I had tried to do for six years without any success, the Lord had done in an instant and without my help.

It got better. "So, that's what we will value your house at, and all your arrearages will be forgiven." I was flabbergasted and speechless. "Is your interest rate okay?" If I'd had my wits about me, I would have said no, but I couldn't even think straight while trying to digest what had just happened. I simply stuttered a "Yes." She concluded the meeting, while the judge and her newly-minted associate remained in speechless shock. She ended with a few more pleasantries and wished us well. She promised to get the paperwork to us in a couple of weeks. That was it. There was no music, no fireworks, no theatrics. There was just God's will being done, as He had promised. The walls of Jericho fell. Two million dollars of debt gone! What an awesome God we serve!

The lender's attorney was true to her word. The paperwork she promised was a four-page letter that explained our future obligation—which was simply that we had to keep the loan for a year and not be delinquent. It also had our new principal balance. The last page required our signatures. That was it. I kept a copy of the letter as a memorial to what God had done. After more than six years of having that foreclosure monkey on my back, we were done. No lawyer, no consultant could have done that. In fact, the ones we had hired to help us were more surprised than we were at what the bank had done. None of them had ever heard of such a thing.

I would like to mention two additional items of importance. The first is that, when we were preparing to build our house, it was a miracle how we had gotten the largest waterfront lot in our neighborhood. I won't go into the details here. Then, after we bought the lot, my wife and I asked her pastor, Colin Braithwaite, to anoint the lot and acknowledge what God had done for us. Now, mind you, I wasn't "in the church" at the time, but our Father who knows the end from the beginning, knew the plans He had for us. I believe He honored us because we honored Him. I plan on asking Him when we meet face to face.

The second thing is what I learned about how American government and big business collude. The foreclosure tsunami that swept across America and the world in 2008 was anticipated, if not planned. As with most things in this country, it disproportionally affected the African American community and stripped our community of accumulated wealth that had taken generations to build. We are still suffering from the fallout today.

In the process of fighting to save my home, working with attorneys and consultants, and having to go to court for other cases, I saw behind the curtain. It is far too complicated to go into detail here, but in a nutshell, state jurisdictions and government officials knew that the way mortgage loans had been marketed, originated, structured, and recorded was fraudulent.[10] Officials also knew that if they did what was right, then they would implicate themselves and lose credibility and money. So, they did nothing. It wasn't about the interests of the people, but about self-preservation and maintaining the status quo. While in court on another case, not my own, I overheard the mortgage bank's attorneys tell the judge that they could not prove that they owned the property they were foreclosing on! The judge asked them what they were going to do, and they told him, they didn't know. The situation was resolved with the bank never having to tell the truth and the court going along with it. This happened right in front of me!

During that time, millions of Americans lost trillions of dollars. African Americans, in particular, lost trillions of dollars in generational wealth as their homes were foreclosed, and all of this happened while an African American was in the highest office in the land. What happened is said to have been the greatest transfer of wealth in human history. My disappointment ran deep, as my hope faded in a political system and the people at its head. No matter what their skin color was, the system was corrupt, and it corrupted those who became a part of it. The lesson learned was simple: trust God, not the paper money that the slogan is printed on. He is our only help.

> Don't put your confidence in powerful people; there is no help for you there. When they breathe their last, they return to the earth, and all their plans die with them. But joyful are those who have the God of Israel as their helper, whose hope is in the LORD their God.
>
> —*Psalm 146:3–5 NLT*

Still, my home had been saved and we were ecstatic. That same day, after we had met with the bank and gotten the good news, we went to visit our daughter for a parent-teacher weekend at Pine Forge Academy. At Friday evening prayer, I gave my testimony through tears of joy. I don't think I was able to tell the whole story. I was not ashamed as other grown men cried along with me—Pastor George Thornton, an old college friend, being one of them. I have always considered that day to be a Red Sea experience. I was hemmed in on all sides. I had to rely solely on God. I was powerless and helpless, but I was not hopeless. We never are when we trust in God. Amen!

CHAPTER 8

The Narrow Road

✝ *Enter ye in at the strait gate: for wide is the gate, and broad is the way, that leadeth to destruction, and many there be which go in thereat: Because strait is the gate, and narrow is the way, which leadeth unto life, and few there be that find it.*

—MATTHEW 7:13–14 KJV

O*nce that trial, the threat of foreclosure* on my house, was behind me, I started looking for opportunities to make money. That was back in 2014 and after everything that had happened, I wanted to make up for lost time. In my garage was a stockpile of several hundred copies of the two books I had written. Their retail value was close to $200,000—as my cousin Morris used to say, "Whole American dollars." I needed to start selling those books to make ends meet, but I was impressed by the Holy Spirit that it was not the right thing to do. In fact, I was impressed to get rid of them the same way I had disposed of my occult library.

Now, mind you, these were copies of the books I had written and paid for myself. This was a very difficult decision for me to make, and I struggled with it for some time, but the impression was unmistakable. The books were not complimentary to God and the teachings of Christianity. In fact, I now consider them blasphemous. They went directly against what the Bible taught. In them were beliefs that promoted everything from evolution to space aliens. Atlantis and Kemet and everything in between were expounded upon in those two books. They were full of lies and demonic deceptions.

No, they had to go.

The Holy Spirit brought to my mind a couple of incidents that took place in the writing of the books that I could not ignore. My wife, Cassandra, would tell me time and time again as she read my first novel, *The Genocide Files*, that I did not write that book. I was always puzzled by her statement and, to be truthful, a little irritated because I couldn't quite understand what she meant. Although, I also had often felt that writing it was too easy. I never experienced the infamous writer's block that so many other writers have encountered. On the contrary, the story and writing of the book flowed effortlessly.

I remember one morning when the book was nearly completed. I wanted to do a poem of dedication to the people who were nearest and dearest to me. It was a poem to my wife, mother, and daughters. As I started to write the poem, the words began to "magically" flow. As the words hit the page, I was surprised. I literally thought, *Am I writing this?* My hands were typing, but it didn't feel like the words were coming from me. It was like someone was writing for me. I cannot explain it any other way.

Since then, I have heard famous musicians and actors speak of this same type of experience, called channeling. In very basic terms, channeling is speaking to and seeking help from supposed spirits of the dead. Movies have made light of mediums who hold séances around a table in a darkened room with unsuspecting people as the medium goes into a trance. However, channeling spirits is not make-believe. It is practiced in many cultures and by many famous people. Some of them have said publicly, it is the cause of their success. Shirley MacLaine, Denzel Washington, and Loretta Lynn have all expressed their belief in communicating with spirits. It is an age-old practice that thrives in today's culture.

I had unsuspectingly indulged in the same practice while writing the book and the poem. The poem was succinct and beautiful, and it was completed in nearly 15 minutes with multiple stanzas. I was amazed at what "I" had written. I began to think that I had more talent than I had given myself credit for—I now know that it wasn't just me doing the writing. My wife, through the Holy Spirit, had been telling me that all along, "You didn't write this book." A friend told me the same thing. I had two witnesses. They were right. I had help from an ungodly muse.

Later, I understood what Cassandra had been telling me, but I wasn't sure she even understood the full implication of her words. I would come to know that the supernatural forces that we allow into our lives can take control of us in a very real sense. An unseen hand can guide our thinking and our actions, even without us giving it our direct consent. That is a frightening thought, but it is true.

The Bible tells us of many such instances of demon influence or outright demon possession, but that fact is easy to dismiss or ignore. In our ignorance, we scoff at things that we cannot see and do not understand. In our arrogance, we think that the things we see happening to others will not happen to us. Both of those attitudes are dangerous in the world we inhabit. Spiritual things are spiritually discerned, and nothing happens by accident. For certain, the enemy influences us to do wrong, but that is just the beginning of his power. Demon possession is just as real today as it was in Christ's time. Early in Christ's ministry, He grappled with demons. What follows occurred in a synagogue of all places!

> Then they went into Capernaum, and immediately on the Sabbath He entered the synagogue and taught. And they were astonished at His teaching, for He taught them as one having authority, and not as the scribes. Now there was a man in their synagogue with an unclean spirit. And he cried out, saying, "Let us alone! What have we to do with You, Jesus of Nazareth? Did You come to destroy us? I know who You are—the Holy One of God!" But Jesus rebuked him, saying, "Be quiet, and come out of him!" And when the unclean spirit had convulsed him and cried out with a loud voice, he came out of him. Then they were all amazed, so that they questioned among themselves, saying, "What is this? What new doctrine is this? For with authority He commands even the unclean spirits, and they obey Him.
>
> —*Mark 1:21–27 NKJV*

Christ, with a few simple words, exorcised the evil spirit from the man. But how did the poor man get into his situation in the first place? The same way all of us do: step-by-step. Ellen White, a well-known Christian writer, shares her perspective on the man's circumstances:

> *The secret cause of the affliction that had made this man a fearful spectacle to his friends and a burden to himself was in his own life. He had been fascinated by the pleasures of sin, and had thought to make life a grand carnival. He did not dream of becoming a terror to the world and the reproach of his family. He thought his time could be spent in innocent folly. But once in the downward path, his feet rapidly descended. Intemperance and frivolity perverted the noble attributes of his nature, and Satan took*

absolute control of him. Remorse came too late. When he would have sacrificed wealth and pleasure to regain his lost manhood, he had become helpless in the grasp of the evil one. He had placed himself on the enemy's ground, and Satan had taken possession of all his faculties. The tempter had allured him with many charming presentations; but when once the wretched man was in his power, the fiend became relentless in his cruelty, and terrible in his angry visitations. So it will be with all who yield to evil; the fascinating pleasure of their early career ends in the darkness of despair or the madness of a ruined soul.[11]

One small step at a time can bring anyone to disaster. It pains me to think of all the friends I have lost to the drug scourge of the seventies and eighties. Young men and young women with bright futures, who came from good homes, and who lost it all one toke at time or one drink at a time. Even though some of them would recover from prostitution and prison, the pain and suffering of those lost years can never be erased. Others would not be so fortunate. They would die in prison, on the streets of D.C., or in mental institutions, not even knowing their own names or what they had lost. I witnessed the effect these generational curses had on families and on our community, in shortened lives and unfulfilled potential. How it must break our Father's heart. And in each case, the devil smiled at his handiwork. That would have been the fate of the unnamed sufferer at Capernaum if not for the compassion of Jesus. Once you are in the devil's snare, it takes a miracle to get you out.

Resisting the Principalities and Powers

Many of you reading this have experienced similar miracles, although maybe not as dramatic. I have. I share this experience with reluctance and after serious prayer. I share it because people need to understand that we are fighting not against flesh and blood enemies, but against principalities, powers, and evil spirits. When we tread on forbidden ground, as I have done, we open ourselves to those same evil forces. They are given access to our minds and bodies by our actions, not necessarily by our consent.

God gives us grace, but we still must choose. The warfare that we are in has rules of engagement that we need to be aware of as much as possible. The Bible helps us to understand how this warfare is waged. Through serious study of the Bible and with God's absolute power, we are better prepared to understand and defeat the enemy.

I was lying in bed one night trying to drift off to sleep. I turned on my side with my face toward the bedroom window. It was then that I heard a familiar voice inside my head. He whispered, "Don't be afraid, he's leaving you." I was puzzled, but in the very next instant, I saw an enormous apparition leave my direction and pass through the closed window to the outside of my house. I was scared to death! I knew that it had left me on the command of the Most High, and I was relieved but shocked by what I had just witnessed. I did not feel any different and I could not tell any difference in my thinking, but maybe that is how possession and oppression work sometimes. It feels like you; it is part of you. Wow—scary, isn't it?

We make one decision at a time, bit by bit and moment by moment, just as I had done. As I said before, I have read and heard about famous athletes, actors, musicians, and personalities making bargains with the devil. I have no doubt that those things have happened. After all, Satan tempted Jesus in the wilderness in the same way. He offered Jesus all the kingdoms of the world if Christ would just worship him. Christ was the exception; the devil tempts the rest of us with trinkets. We will only realize the true value of our life when we measure it by how much Jesus paid for it. We sell our souls for discount, bargain basement prices. So many of us look at the wealth and the fame. We see the mansions and the cars, not realizing that they represent the same poisonous fruit that Eve ate. Be smart and remember that whatever the devil offers you here is not worth passing up heaven for. I learned that the hard way. As Ellen White writes:

Satan is constantly at work, but few have any idea of his activity and subtlety. The people of God must be prepared to withstand the wily foe. It is this resistance that Satan dreads. He knows better than we do the limit of his power and how easily he can be overcome if we resist and face him. Through divine strength the weakest saint is more than a match for him and all his angels, and if brought to the test [the weakest saint] would be able to prove his superior power. Therefore Satan's step is noiseless, his movements stealthy, and his batteries masked. He does not venture to show himself openly, lest he arouse the Christian's dormant energies and send him [or her] to God in prayer.[12]

I had been chasing after the things of this world, disregarding truths I had been taught from the time I was a child. I stepped on toes and made wrong decisions based on temporal gain. I crossed the line when I knew better. All of those things put my soul in jeopardy and put me inside the enemy's camp. The enemy took advantage. There are many others who've had similar experiences.

The devil is constantly at work filling up our minds and our time with distractions and diversions. I'd grown so accustomed to his distractions, that I felt lost without them. My friends were in the same boat with me. I finally began to learn that everything we watch, hear, and participate in either helps us or hurts us. Those influences place us in God's camp or in the enemy's camp. Television, social media, movies, music, sports, politics, fashion, and the list goes on—all these things engage the mind and affect our reasoning ability. We must guard the avenues to our mind, at all cost. We must always strive for the moral high ground. As the news screams daily, we live in perilous times, and we must put on the whole armor of God, always!

All those things seem appealing and harmless when we are enjoying life, or in card game vernacular, sitting at the table. But when it is time to cash in the chips, well, that is when we find if it was all worth it. Many have learnt that it wasn't. Again, that was the path I was on. With my books and my business, I was headed for wealth and fame, but what I would have lost would have been far more than what I would have gained. Yet, it all started so innocently, in a church with a sermon that the enemy used to fuel misdirection and blind me to God's plan for my life. I also helped too by twisting the preacher's words to meet my own desires. The Bible expressed it this way:

> And remember, our Lord's patience gives people time to be saved. This is what our beloved brother Paul also wrote to you with the wisdom God gave him— speaking of these things in all of his letters. Some of his comments are hard to understand, and those who are ignorant and unstable have twisted his letters to mean something quite different, just as they do with other parts of Scripture. And this will result in their destruction.
>
> —*2 Peter 3:15–16 NLT*

Standing Firm in Human Company

The Christian walk was a daily struggle. Once I was baptized and had made a public stand for Christ, things didn't just suddenly change. I still had problems. I still had my same neighbors, friends, and acquaintances. Many of the people I knew and hung out with did not understand my conversion, the "new" me. They were still doing the same things and enjoying them. It wasn't just something they did—it was who they were. With Christ, the change occurs from the inside out. At first, to be honest, I missed the social events and the hanging out. With seducing intentions, friends in my neighborhood would tell me about all the fun and the wild parties that were going on.

I'm sure they wondered if my conversion was real or if I was just momentarily enamored. Did I miss hanging out at the marina, on the boats? Did I miss the parties and the nightlife? I had been in their mix for years—some felt I would certainly be back. It took a while for them to believe that my new way of living was for real. From time to time, I would drop in at one of their boats. "You want a drink, Nate?" was the inevitable question, and my answer was always the same, "No." We would chat awkwardly for a while. They would share the latest gossip and I would try to get a word in about how good God had been to me, but there was no real interest in hearing what the other had to say. We were in different worlds which were opposed to each other. The estrangement could not be reconciled. I would always leave with a silent prayer for each of them and be thankful that I had gotten off the merry-go-round.

Many of my neighborhood friends had good jobs and nice houses. They were often traveling and partying. Money was not an object in their circles, and at one time, that had been the case with me. Super Bowl trips, condos in the Bahamas, private yachting excursions in Bermuda, these were all typical. It was always something. They had to fill their time with things to do as if they were afraid to just do nothing. Maybe they were afraid. It is in the quiet moments that you can hear the still, small voice. The voice that tells you, "This is the way, walk ye in it" (Isaiah 30:21 KJV). So, to quiet that voice, you keep busy. That is what I believe my friends and neighbors were really doing.

The Bible also tells us, "Know ye not that the friendship of the world is enmity with God?" and it's true. Once you realize the emptiness of living a selfish and worldly life, you don't want to go back. Christ came to give us life and to give us life more abundantly, for now and for eternity. That is something that you cannot just tell people, you must live it out in front of them. That is the best way to convince people that you've changed; that is what Christ did.

As I started to do church-related activities to help others, I had less time to hang out with my old friends. We were still cordial, but our interests and activities had diverged. I would get the occasional call telling me that someone was sick or that something had happened. The call would end with the not so veiled request for prayer. I would pray for them, but even those calls became fewer in number. So, I resolved to pray for all of them anyway, and I still do. I will share an example of what I mean here. This happened after I had joined a church.

Rick, a friend and neighbor, called to tell me that a mutual friend, Arnell, who owned a nice establishment in Southern Maryland, had been in a terrible car accident after leaving a boat party at the marina. His truck flipped over with him inside while he was legally intoxicated. This was the third major accident he'd had in a short period of time. Fortunately, he survived the incident. A couple of weeks later he attended a church in Clinton where my neighbor is a pastor. When the minister made the appeal, Arnell went to the front, just like I had done. I had tremendous hope for him and prayed for him, but after a short while, he fell back into his old ways. That happens a lot.

The devil never gives up. In his finite power, he is relentless. Fortunately, God doesn't give up either, and He has infinite resources and power. He knows what is best for His children and how to bless His children. Every promise in God's word is true and He stands behind each and every one. I would soon learn that every promise that God makes, He is ready, willing, and able to fulfill.

CHAPTER 9

Restoration!

✝   *And I will restore to you the years that the locust hath eaten, the*
cankerworm, and the caterpiller, and the palmerworm, my great
army which I sent among you.

And ye shall eat in plenty, and be satisfied, and praise the name
of the LORD your God, that hath dealt wondrously with you:
and my people shall never be ashamed.

—JOEL 2:25-26 KJV

M **y youth had evaporated. My young adult** years were behind me. The years of my middle age were nearly spent and
I felt like I was starting over. The luster of life had worn off

and I was left with the reality. I felt like a failure except for one reason: God. I had to make new friends and start over in business, but now I was on God's side and in His grace. Still, it was a difficult rebuilding process, but as these changes were taking place in my life, the economy slowly improved. Although my business was still struggling, I was slowly beginning to close deals. It all started when I connected with an old acquaintance, Al Barber, who was working as an assessor for the District of Columbia government.

Al was working at D.C.'s tax assessor office and had started researching probate cases while there. He developed a system to find and engage the personal representatives of the deceased estates. We worked out a plan and it fell to me to make the calls and personal contacts. The cold-calling and follow-up took time, patience, and consistency. It was hard work because I hadn't done cold canvassing in years, but the deals were consistent and they were good, meaning the returns were much more than the average transaction.

With each listing, I quickly developed a core group of cash buyers. All of them were foreigners, and none of them had less than several million dollars in cash money to invest. This was a welcome change for me. Working with cash buyers made my deals easy, by comparison to what I had been used to. Most probate properties needed substantial renovation, and as a probate specialist, I often represented both the buyer and the seller. That was a double commission. While other realtors were struggling to survive, my business began to pick up steadily. This was all in the Lord's timing and in His purpose for me.

Like that of so many others, my Christian journey is filled with missteps and setbacks but also victories and triumphs. Perhaps unique about my experience is that, as I progressed through each valley and up each mountain, I was able to chronicle my experiences. I did this at first by memory and by rehashing them repeatedly, and then by keeping a written chronicle of them. As I did that, I soon realized that many of the events detailed in the Bible paralleled my personal experiences. I could see God working in my life as He had worked in the lives of the Israelites and other Biblical figures. I began to understand in a real and personal way how Christian character is developed; the process of sanctification, and what my role and duties as a Christian were.

I have had my Red Sea experience and my Jericho wall experience. In each one, I learned something new about God and about myself. When Moses led the children of Israel to the shore of the Red Sea, they were hemmed in. They couldn't go right or left, and they couldn't turn back. They had to go forward. But there was just that one thing—millions of tons of water blocked their way. Pharaoh's army was behind them, and the sea was in front of them. Why would God place them in such a position?

> Be still, and know that I am God; I will be exalted among the nations, I will be exalted in the earth.
>
> —*Psalm 46:10 NIV*

It is in those still moments that God can get our full attention. Being still has been one of the most challenging things for me. It requires trust and patience. It requires prayer and faith. It is humbling and, any way you slice it, it is just hard. The thing is, it is necessary for the Christian's walk with God. It has been in mine.

Like the children of Israel, I was hemmed in when the economy collapsed and my business failed. I was hemmed in when my house was headed for certain foreclosure and my family and I would have been homeless and dependent on the kindness of others. With all my vaunted experience and skill in real estate, I was helpless. All I could do was rely on God, His tender mercies, His loving kindness. The Red Sea was in front of me. I was powerless, but God was all-powerful. At His command, my Red Sea parted, and I walked through on dry land. The miracle was obvious, and just as clear was the fact that I had done absolutely nothing to accomplish the saving of my family's home.

But here is my sad confession: I still had a one percent doubt that God had been the one to do it. The enemy filled my head with questions that undermined the miracle. Forget the fact that God had instructed me to walk around my house seven times. Forget the fact that the attorneys I hired had never seen anything like it before. I still wondered if it was all Him. After all, I had been the one to hire all those attorneys. Maybe God used some of the filings they submitted to effect the outcome. That was probably the same attitude that some of the Israelites had when leaving Egypt. They had witnessed miracle after miracle. They had seen the pillar of fire. They had been spared the plagues and there was the Passover of their first born. The problem with miracles is that oftentimes people ignore them or diminish them. I know this sounds crazy, but it is true. Time and time again, God performed miracles for the Israelites during their wilderness journey, and time and time again they rebelled, disobeyed, or disregarded Him.

But before you begin to point fingers; we all do the same thing. Every day when you wake up, when you speak to your loved ones, and when you take a deep breath, you should recognize and thank God, without whom none of those things are possible. You might say that you do thank Him, and I won't argue with you, God knows. Let me just say that my experiences pointed out where I had fallen short. I can recite so many miracles I have seen or experienced in my life, but I cringe to think how I lived my life after experiencing each one. In most cases, I continued doing the same thing. I continued on the same path.

God had displayed His mighty power, but there is more to God than power. There is more to the Christian walk than obedience out of fear.

There must be a daily surrender, a daily communion. Relationship building takes time and effort; it is the same with our relationship with Christ. In retrospect, I understood that what I was experiencing was simply Christian growing pains. A child has to drink milk before he can digest solid food. Just as the Israelites had to walk in the wilderness, so did I. So do you. Relationship building is the process of growing in love.

There are times when you are sincerely seeking to do God's will. You are going to church and doing everything that you feel you are required to do, yet still bad things happen. You get sick, a loved one dies, or you lose your good paying job. Sometimes all of those things happen at once. As one of my church elders, Orlan Johnson, often says, "You are either going into a storm, in a storm, or coming out of a storm." Storms are a part of this life, especially the Christian's life.

> I'm not asking you to take them out of the world, but to keep them safe from the evil one. They do not belong to this world any more than I do.
>
> —*John 17:15–16 NLT*

Christ prayed for each of us because He understood that we all experience trials in this life, and He wanted us to be prepared. Trials are not necessarily a punishment; they are an opportunity to grow into the fullness of God. They are an opportunity to glorify God. It helps you to view them as such. The Apostles Peter and Paul also understood this:

> Stand firm against him, and be strong in your faith. Remember that your family of believers all over the world is going through the same kind of suffering you are. In his kindness God called you to share in his eternal glory by means of Christ Jesus. So after you have suffered

a little while, he will restore, support, and strengthen you, and he will place you on a firm foundation.

—*1 Peter 5:9–10 NLT*

Now I want you to know, brothers and sisters, that what has happened to me has actually served to advance the gospel.

—*Philippians 1:12 NIV*

The storms we all go through, the suffering, they strengthen us and help us to promote the gospel through our testimony. We have God's promise that He will restore, support, strengthen, and set us on a firm foundation. The storm I was entering, I did not anticipate and was not prepared for. But God was.

In the summer of 2018, my brother, Ullysee died after a brief illness. We were shocked and devastated. Our church family rallied around us and that softened the blow, but it was still very hard. I had expected Ullysee to fully recover and, when he didn't, I was angry at life and at God. But Ulysses' death was only the beginning of the storm. The waves, wind, lightening, and tumult of my own personal storm were only a few months away. It started with a phone call right before Sabbath.

My doctor called and told me she suspected I had prostate cancer—it was February. I was distraught. This would be my second bout with cancer, and I was afraid. I was an elder at Capitol Hill Seventh-day Adventist Church. I was leading out in my churches' personal ministries department and was working actively to lead souls to Christ. I felt betrayed, again. Remember, I had experienced God's miracles in my life, and I was walking in obedience. I was up at 5 a.m. every morning. I prayed for one hour, fasted two days a week, and read the Bible for an hour each day for devotion. I

also went on the church's prayer line for an hour. I was working to earn
God's favor and not fully realizing that I had it already. It reminds me of
what Paul said.

> I was circumcised when I was eight days old. I am a pure-blooded cit-
> izen of Israel and a member of the tribe of Benjamin—a real Hebrew
> if there ever was one! I was a member of the Pharisees, who demand
> the strictest obedience to the Jewish law.
>
> —*Philippians 3:5 NLT*

In the deep recess of my mind, I thought that by doing all those things I
would be exempt from the pains and trials of life. Christ had been telling
me all along why He came and what I should expect in the Christian life,
but I was unable to hear.

As they approached Jerusalem for the final time, Christ told his disciples
what to expect, but they couldn't hear either:

> I have told you all this so that you may have peace in me. Here on
> earth you will have many trials and sorrows. But take heart, because I
> have overcome the world."
>
> —*John 16:33 NLT*

Christ told me, just as He tells you. Our peace is in Him—we must learn
to rest in Him. My second cancer storm would bring this lesson home
in a way that I will never forget. As I began to come to grips with my
diagnosis and treatment, I had some concerns. I had two physicians. One
was an oncologist, who I had been seeing for twenty years. The other was
my primary physician at the Washington Hospital Center. The latter, Dr.

Davidson, had also been my brother's doctor. I'd had some issues with her bedside manner and had very nearly left her practice. However, I didn't know who else to see at the time, so I continued as her patient. She gave me a referral to a well-known urologist, but I didn't follow up with him. Instead, I started asking around for good doctors. I ended up going with a physician who was at Washington Adventist Hospital in Takoma Park. He was Asian American and very personable. I liked him, and so did my wife. His name was Jonathan R. Dr. R was a Christian and prayed with us. I felt he was the one to go with. The fact that his name was Jonathan; I took as a sign. Jonathan means "God has given."

The biopsy was performed and the results confirmed that I had cancer. Dr. R wasn't sure which approach was best for me but was leaning toward surgery. He wanted me to confer with my hematologist and get his recommendation. Radiation might not kill the cancer and limit future options and chemotherapy was not the typical protocol for my condition. I was inclined to do radiation, but the other factors weighed against it. I spoke with Dr. Anand, my hematologist, and he felt that surgery or radiation wouldn't impact my leukemia. However, he felt that surgery was the best option. Still, I really didn't want to do the surgery. I had never been cut on in my life, so that was my last option to consider.

If I had been praying before, you should have seen me then. I answered every altar call our pastor gave. It got so that one of my friends, also an elder, James Mitchell, commented to me that he knew something was up when I came to the front every week. I was at the Red Sea again, but it wasn't easier—it was harder.

At that point, I consulted with a urologist, Leon Seard, who was a close friend of my wife. Cassandra had grown up with Dr. Seard, and I knew him as well. He concurred with the radiologist. He also recommended some well-known hospitals like Georgetown and Johns Hopkins. He may have even mentioned Washington Hospital Center. Dr. Seard strongly suggested that I at least speak to some of their specialists to see how I felt about what they had to say. It made sense, and it addressed a major concern I had at that time. During this time, I gathered a group of family and church elders to anoint me and to pray for me daily. There was a total of eleven of them. I also asked Christ to pray for me. That made it an even twelve.

Who then will condemn us? No one—for Christ Jesus died for us and was raised to life for us, and he is sitting in the place of honor at God's right hand, pleading for us.

—*Romans 8:34 NLT*

It was time for my regular physical, so I went to my primary care physician, Dr. Davidson. In the treatment room, she sat down across from me, her back toward me, facing the computer. She started with the typical doctor small talk and I responded in kind. As she looked at the screen, it prompted her to ask about my surgery.

She asked, "When is your surgery scheduled?"

She could be intimidating, but I mustered up the courage to say firmly, "It should be sometime next month. I'm still working with the doctor's office to get an exact date."

She turned around from her computer and stared at me with a puzzled look. I knew I was in for a lashing. "What do you mean, you're still talking to the doctor's office? He should have been able to get you in by now!"

There was no use in mincing words, so I told her plainly, "I didn't speak to the doctor you gave me. I got a referral from one of my members at my church. Her husband has a urologist at Washington Adventist Hospital."

She wanted to say something but she didn't. Instead, she took her time before she spoke. I prayed silently. She started, after a deep breath, in a measured and compassionate tone of voice. Looking me in the eye; she didn't blink.

"Mr. Arnold, you're playing with your life. Cancer is nothing to fool around with. As your doctor, I'm looking out for your best interest. The referral I gave you was to the head of our urology department. He is one of the best surgeons on the entire East Coast. Doctors follow a process, we adhere to proven and tested protocols, processes that are measured over time. Stick with the process, it's designed to save your life."

Dr. Davidson was genuinely concerned. Normally, I would have argued with her, but this time I didn't. I took hers as the voice of God speaking directly to me. I listened in a spirit of humility. I knew God had an order and a process by which He works. Davidson reminded me of that. He sets up authorities and powers and expects us to adhere to them as long as they don't conflict with His authority and power.

> Everyone must submit to governing authorities. For all authority comes from God, and those in positions of authority have been placed there by God. So anyone who rebels against authority is rebelling against what God has instituted, and they will be punished.
>
> —*Romans 13:1-2 NLT*

I lifted my head and simply said, "You're right."

She took a moment and turned back to her computer and got the number to the referral she'd given me before. "Here's Dr. Hwang's office number again. Please call his office and tell them that I referred you. I will make sure that they get your lab results. Let me know when you speak to them."

I finished, "Thanks, Doc."

"You're welcome, Mr. Arnold." She smiled as she extended her hand and I took the information and prayed to God that I would be in His will.

How would I handle my previous doctor? I'd had some concerns about Dr. R—not really about him, but about the service I was getting. I felt the care I was currently getting from his office could have been better. Sometimes I couldn't speak to him and would leave a message with the office manager. She always seemed to rush me, and the doctor never seemed to get the messages I left. I had kept quiet and just allowed my uneasiness to simmer. Additionally, the Seventh-day Adventist hospital in Takoma Park was scheduled to close the month after my surgery. I didn't like that, even though the new hospital Dr. R would be working from was state-of-the-art. It was located in White Oak.

I was concerned about the continuity and quality of my care. Of course, I didn't tell my primary physician all those things. I planned to make an appointment with her referral. The enemy was putting all sorts of things in my head, and I was having second thoughts. Maybe I really didn't need surgery. Maybe I could go the holistic route. My fear was getting the better of me, and I began to complain rather than pray. I prayed then as I headed home. "Father, I'm afraid. I don't know what to do. Help me Father, my life is in your hands. Guide me in the way I should go. My eyes are watching you."

On the drive home, I felt calm for the first time in a while. I turned down the street heading to my house and saw a neighbor, Richard. I hadn't seen Richard in a while. He was jogging as I drove past him. I remembered that he'd had prostate cancer some years before, and I decided that I should speak to him. I turned the car around and slowed down beside him. We began to talk, and I told him what was going on. He shared some of his experiences with me. I was encouraged. He then told me that his brother, Claude, recently had prostate surgery and that he had gone to a surgeon at Washington Hospital Center. It was the same doctor my physician had just recommended. Now, that doctor's name was also Jonathan! But it gets better. Claude's wife was a surgical nurse, and she worked with that same doctor. God's timing is always perfect.

Later, I called Richard to get his brother's number, and Cassandra and I spoke to him and his wife, Barbara, on the phone. As we talked, Barbara went into great detail about the surgery and what to expect. She had worked with Dr. Jonathan Hwang for years and told me he had personally performed over three thousand surgeries. I knew my prayer had been answered. I knew I was in God's will. What else can I say—this was not another Red Sea experience but a Jordan River experience where my feet actually got wet.

I made an appointment with Dr. Jonathan Hwang, and all the previous misgivings I'd had were assuaged. My wife took her notebook into the consultation, and we asked every question we could think of. He answered them to our satisfaction. Their procedures were somewhat different from my first doctors, and they had a much higher success rate for nerve sparing. Dr. Hwang was the one who would do my surgery.

When I had my surgery in July, I was still scared but I knew I was in God's favor . I knew because I had asked God if I really had to do this. I asked Him what would happen if I didn't have the surgery. It was not an answer that I wanted to hear. Through my fear, I reflected on God's promises as we drove to the hospital. My wife, Pastor Peeler, and Pastor Wade were all at the hospital with me. The pastors prayed for me, and I thank God for their compassion and intercession.

As I was taken by gurney into the preparatory surgery area, I was amazed at the number of people having surgery that morning. I asked the nurse attending me if this was typical, and she assured me it was. A chaplain came and prayed for me—he had been contacted by Saundra Austin. He prayed a quick prayer and stayed long enough to greet a couple of people he knew on the surgery team. It seemed to be business as usual to everyone, to everyone but me. A young, White nurse came to find a vein for the anesthesia drip. She punctured my hand without good results. She seemed frazzled, and that caused me as much discomfort as the wound she inflicted on my hand. A senior, Black nurse noticed what was going on and tactfully offered to help. She chose a vein in my arm and quickly accomplished her task. Like airplanes on a runway tarmac, patients' names were called, and soon I was rolled into the operating room. The room was antiseptic white and metallic silver. As I recall, there were two men attending me, and one of them explained the process. They placed the drip in my arm, told me what to expect, and that was it. I don't remember anything else after that.

The next thing I do remember is waking up, my wife beside me talking to one of the nurses. I was alive! Thank you, Jesus! My surgery didn't take as long as they had expected and I was doing well, but that gave me time to reflect. I'd never had surgery before and I'd never spent a night in a hospital. I was in unfamiliar territory. I was not invincible nor was I immortal. Illness has a way of putting life's priorities into perspective. God is in charge and I was truly on a walk of faith. I realized that every breath I took was a gift of grace. He would prove to me that His grace is sufficient.

The truth is, the worst experience up to that point was the young nurse hitting the dry vein. I was thankful I had chosen that hospital. Washington Hospital Center had a special recovery area for privacy. I spent the night there. It was a private area separate from the main hospital, and I had my own nurse. This area was reserved for dignitaries or anyone who could pay the fee. Edward Kennedy had spent the night there after a surgery he'd had. My primary physician made sure I knew about it and told me to insist on recovering there. I was thankful I had kept her as my doctor. It pays to be obedient to God.

My family came by to visit, and I could see the expression of relief on their faces. I let them know I was fine and should be home the next day. The night went well and I didn't feel bad. I couldn't eat much, and I threw up once from some medicine they gave me, but the worst of it was the catheter. Could I make it a week with the catheter? I had my doubts. My wife spent the night in the hospital with me and slept soundly. By 11:00 a.m. the next day I was being prepped for the trip home. Fortunately, my wife was off from work and helped me with everything. Cassandra had been by my side through everything and I was more than just grateful—I was humbled. God knew who I would need to help me in those moments. A Scripture from Proverbs reminded me of His providence. I praise Him and thank her.

> Fathers can give their sons an inheritance of houses and wealth, but only the LORD can give an understanding wife.
>
> —*Proverbs 19:14 NLT*

As I write this, it has been slightly over a year since my surgery. God is also writing my testimony. He promised to bring me through my surgery and recovery with flying colors, and that is exactly what He did. My testimony is simply this: God is faithful and nothing is impossible for Him. Christ's sacrifice, His blood is why I have overcome.

> And they overcame him by the blood of the Lamb, and by the word of their testimony; and they loved not their lives unto the death.
>
> —*Revelation 12:11 KJV*

In His Kindness

Many things were going on throughout the six months of my diagnosis, surgery, and recovery. I had to do diagnostic tests regularly. After each one, there was the difficult process of waiting for the results. Had the cancer spread? How bad was it? Was it localized? Would I live? Would I die? Was God really talking to me? Could I believe God? Why was my faith so weak? All of those things were going through my mind.

During that time, a particular incident stands out. A deaconess at my church, Sylvia Williams, had a son about my age who was diagnosed with the same type of cancer I had, and she kept me posted on how well he was doing. I was encouraged by her reports. Additionally, more than a few men in my church came to me to tell me of their own experience with prostate cancer. I was surprised by how many there were. Oftentimes men don't discuss things like prostate cancer openly. This is especially true of Black men, even though African American men have the highest rate of prostate cancer in the entire world.

Through my recovery process, I had good days and bad days—not physically, but mentally. Physically, I was improving daily. But the enemy preys on fear and doubt, and the more you entertain those things the worse it gets. I wasn't sleeping well or eating much. In fact, during the period right before and after surgery, I lost 49 pounds. Truthfully, I needed to lose the weight, but it took the cancer diet to do it. I would not recommend that to anyone.

I was approaching the time for my next diagnostic test when Sylvia announced on the church's prayer line that her son, who had been doing so well, didn't look like he was going to make it. I was shocked. I asked her what had happened. She explained that he had not been telling her the truth. He'd had advanced cancer and didn't want his family to know the real story. She only found out after his doctor called her into his office and spoke to her directly. Sylvia was devastated. Her son only had about a week to live. With my own test looming and with me feeling so close to his situation, that was one of my bad days.

But God already knew what would happen and had prepared me. Sometime before that, I had been impressed to start journaling. As I was going through some of my old entries, I saw how God had worked in my life so often and so profoundly. I recalled miracle after miracle of what He had done for me. I had not forgotten the miracles, but I had taken them for granted. I realized how unthankful I had been and how much I had complained. I asked for forgiveness and it sometimes seemed that was all I was doing; asking for forgiveness. I never knew that the Christian walk would be so hard and that grace was so abundant. Through it all, one thought stood out for me: If I could not trust God here, I would not get the chance to trust Him in heaven. If I could not walk with Him here, how could I walk with Him in heaven? No matter what, I knew I couldn't give up, I couldn't let go; I had entered into my Jacob experience, wrestling with God.

This left Jacob all alone in the camp, and a man came and wrestled with him until the dawn began to break. When the man saw that he would not win the match, he touched Jacob's hip and wrenched it out of its socket. Then the man said, "Let me go, for the dawn is breaking!" But Jacob said, "I will not let you go unless you bless me." "What is your name?" the man asked. He replied, "Jacob." "Your name will no longer be Jacob," the man told him. "From now on you will be called Israel, because you have fought with God and with men and have won.

—*Genesis 32:24-28 NLT*

I thought back to an incident before my surgery. One night, I was crying out to God on my outdoor patio, the moonlight beaming through the trees and reflecting off the water. Knowing that my life hung in the balance, I prayed to my Father. With anguished tears rolling down my face, as much as I wanted to live, I knew the decision was in my Father's hands. I surrendered to Him, and the words of declaration came from my tear-stained lips, "Lord, thy will be done." No sooner had I audibly uttered those words when I heard God tell me that He was giving my life back to me. I praised Him with all my heart. At that moment, the heaviness I felt instantly left me, and I cried tears of joy. It was my Gethsemane experience. God had always been God, but at that instant He also became Lord. At that moment, I gained insight into the distinction.

In the relationship God has with us, He has established a covenant. Central to His covenant for us is His grace, love, mercy, protection, and the list goes on. Central to our worship of Him is our love, obedience, faithfulness, consecration, praise, and the list continues. He is God, and He is sovereign; we are His creation, His children, His redeemed.

> I will answer them before they even call to me. While they are still talking about their needs, I will go ahead and answer their prayers!
>
> —*Isaiah 65:24 (NLT)*

I had often wondered what it would take to make it through the time of trouble coming upon the world in the last days. I had often prayed about it. I had lived a pampered life and had learned to take so many things for granted. I knew I wasn't ready for real privation, for the pain and suffering prophesied in God's word about the last days. How does one get prepared for suffering, death, calamities, and destruction?

Through my own experience, I was beginning to understand that it would take a consecrated life and a living faith—a walk with God that, in all my religious zeal, I was still missing. I was beginning to understand what sanctification really is. It is a daily surrender to the will of God and a daily consecration of my total being. It is a growing, a trusting, a relationship-building process. And it is God's work. He is the Husbandman, and we are the seed.

Sanctification results in our personal testimony. That process is our experience—all of our experience in our Christian walk. Our prayers, praise, faith, perseverance, every valley we go through, every summit we mount, every season of despair and every heartfelt hallelujah is chronicled here on earth and will be extolled in heaven. And it is all due to His kindness and for His glory. My experience, through my brother's death and my second cancer trial, helped me to better understand this reality. A Christian writer put it this way:

The germination of the seed represents the beginning of spiritual life, and the development of the plant is a beautiful figure of Christian growth. As in nature, so in grace; there can be no life without growth. The plant must either grow or die. As its growth is silent and imperceptible, but continuous, so is the development of the Christian life. At every stage of development our life may be perfect; yet if God's purpose for us is fulfilled, there will be continual advancement. Sanctification is the work of a lifetime. As our opportunities multiply, our experience will enlarge, and our knowledge increase. We shall become strong to bear responsibility, and our maturity will be in proportion to our privileges.

The plant grows by receiving that which God has provided to sustain its life. It sends down its roots into the earth. It drinks in the sunshine, the dew, and the rain. It receives the life-giving properties from the air. So the Christian is to grow by co-operating with the divine agencies. Feeling our helplessness, we are to improve all the opportunities granted us to gain a fuller experience. As the plant takes root in the soil, so we are to take deep root in Christ. As the plant receives the sunshine, the dew, and the rain, we are to open our hearts to the Holy Spirit. The work is to be done "not by might, nor by power, but by My Spirit, saith the Lord of hosts." Zechariah 4:6. If we keep our minds stayed upon Christ, He will come unto us "as the rain, as the latter and former rain unto the earth." Hosea 6:3. As the Sun of Righteousness, He will arise upon us "with healing in His wings." Malachi 4:2. We shall "grow as the lily." We shall "revive as the corn, and grow as the vine." Hosea 14:5, 7. By constantly relying upon Christ as our personal Saviour, we shall grow up into Him in all things who is our head.[13]

Sanctification is this daily process, like a plant growing from seed to its fullness. I couldn't understand or appreciate that process fully then, but with time I began to understand. God is patient and faithful to bring us to our fullness in Him. I can appreciate that even if I don't fully understand it. The Apostle Paul expounds on the sanctification process in Ephesians 1:16-18 (NLT). He said:

I have not stopped thanking God for you. I pray for you constantly, asking God, the glorious Father of our Lord Jesus Christ, to give you spiritual wisdom and insight so that you might grow in your knowledge of God. I pray that your hearts will be flooded with light so that you can understand the confident hope he has given to those he called—his holy people who are his rich and glorious inheritance.

An aspect of spiritual wisdom and insight allows us to understand that every single experience we go through can teach us eternal lessons. There are no such things as luck or chance. None of our experience should be taken for granted or at face value. Each experience has both superficial and deeper meanings. Sanctification is understanding this truth.

When God Calls

> Now Samuel did not yet know the LORD, neither was the word of
> the LORD yet revealed unto him. And the LORD called Samuel
> again the third time. And he arose and went to Eli, and said, Here am
> I; for thou didst call me. And Eli perceived that the LORD had called
> the child. Therefore Eli said unto Samuel, Go, lie down: and it shall
> be, if he call thee, that thou shalt say, Speak, LORD; for thy servant
> heareth. So Samuel went and lay down in his place.
>
> —*1 Samuel 3:7-9 KJV*

Each one of us has the call of God upon our lives—I am no different.
What is different is how we respond to that call; if we hear it and understand what it is, but most importantly if we answer it. Did I hear my
Father's third call and would I answer it? My earliest experiences had been
saturated with the injustices of life and American racism in particular. I
could recite incident upon incident of injustice, each one a brick in the
wall of separation between my fellow men and by consequence God. The
equation is simple; sin separates us from God and consequently from each
other. No man can love God yet hate his fellow man. Racism is sin and
those who embrace it must repent of it and seek reconciliation with those
they have wronged and with God. This is not optional. In fact, this is a
prerequisite for forgiveness.

> If a man say, I love God, and hateth his brother, he is a liar: for he
> that loveth not his brother whom he hath seen, how can he love God
> whom he hath not seen? And this commandment have we from him,
> That he who loveth God love his brother also. (1 John 4:20-21 KJV)

> But I say unto you, That whosoever is angry with his brother without
> a cause shall be in danger of the judgment: and whosoever shall say
> to his brother, Raca, shall be in danger of the council: but whosoever
> shall say, Thou fool, shall be in danger of hell fire. Therefore if thou
> bring thy gift to the altar, and there rememberest that thy brother
> hath ought against thee; Leave there thy gift before the altar, and go
> thy way; first be reconciled to thy brother, and then come and offer
> thy gift.
>
> —*Matthew 5:22-24*

Those twin truths, the first by John and the second by Jesus, were a two-edged sword clearly exposing my problem and cutting through my hypocrisy. The wall that separated me from my fellow men, no matter the cause, separated me also from God. "God forgive me and cleanse me from my sins," was my prayer. It was heartfelt and directed especially at the sin of racism. It was in that moment that I knew something had changed. The calling I had on my life began to come into focus. The experiences I'd had and could never rise above all took on a different understanding. My searching and questioning all made sense.

"Why did you make me a negro?" The simple childhood question that I had asked my loving Father 60 years before, He now answered for me. But the simple question I posed could not be answered simply. It was complicated with a cause and purpose beyond surface comprehension. Our Father loves us too much than to simply pat us on the head and say we will know one day in the sweet bye-and-bye. That question could not have been answered with a simple response. I could not understand it nor would I have appreciated it. The answer took those myriad experiences that I have cited in this book and an understanding into spiritual warfare that could only be granted by God. God's faithfulness and compassion were to be displayed in me and through me. His name will be glorified by His answer. How?

I'm glad you asked. You see, God will have a people that will stand in these last days reflecting His character and honoring His name to a disobedient and unrepenting world. His people will, must, fulfil Christ's commandment in John 13. Christ commanded His followers:

> A new commandment I give unto you, That ye love one another; as I have loved you, that ye also love one another. By this shall all men know that ye are my disciples, if ye have love one to another.
>
> —*John 13:34-35 KJV*

It will be clear that we cannot love God if we don't love one another. This is the calling of all Christians, not just mine. It is especially important for the Seventh-day Adventist Church. Why? Because we profess to "*Keep the commandments of God, and have the testimony of Jesus Christ.*" We applaud ourselves for remembering the Sabbath day when most other Protestant denominations have forgotten it. But this badge of honor must be stripped from us when we so flagrantly disobey Christ's new commandment.

> For whosoever shall keep the whole law, and yet offend in one point, he is guilty of all.
>
> —*James 2:10 KJV*

The commandment to love one another is not part of the decalogue, that is true, yet it is the greatest commandment. It is the intent, the character, of the law and the testimony. We cannot parse it and we dare not ignore it any longer.

Again, Seventh-day Adventists who have been given the prophetic gift, health reform, the sanctuary and three Angel's messages should know this better than anyone else. To whom much is given, much shall be required. Bequeathed to this movement and this generation is the Spirit of prophecy and it is charged with proclaiming the final message to humanity, the three angels' message found in Revelation 14. This generation will not pass until we fulfill our charge, which is to proclaim with a loud voice Christ's imminent return. The realization of those truths and the acceptance of them stretched my prayers and took me out of my comfort zone. Which was more important: Heaven and eternal life, or holding on to the hurts and disappointments of this life?

So, after I prayed for forgiveness for my prejudice, I carefully and humbly asked God what He wanted me to do. I did not have to wait long. I was to write a letter and present it to several men at my church, Capitol Hill. There was no real plan behind the letter other than to come together and discuss race and how it affected us and our church. This was the thing, though: after I had written the letters, I didn't know to whom I was to give them. So, obediently I took the letters to church and held them through Sabbath School. With fear and trembling, I asked the Lord who I was to give them.

I followed the Holy Spirit's leading and handed the first letter to a deacon (I won't mention his name due to the sensitive nature of his work). I explained what it was and I was shocked that he took it, but even more shocking was that I had given it to him in the first place. I didn't know him well and what I did know, made me somewhat apprehensive of him. He was a law enforcement officer working for the FBI and I believed he was a republican, although I had no proof of the latter. I held serious grievances against both of those entities and painted him with the same brush of my prejudice. I could not separate them from him. Those were bricks in my wall that God needed to tear down. Some people say that God has a sense of humor—I think rather He has an unrelenting will to save us and no obstacle that the enemy has erected will stand in His way.

The remaining five letters went to Terrell Danley Jr., my brother-in-law, Mark Washington, Theodore Allen, Josue Pierre, and the last one to receive a letter was Robin Sampson, our head deacon. The letters were handed out in the winter of 2020 before the COVID-19 lockdown and the exacerbation of race relations brought on by the murder of George Floyd. Our first scheduled get-together was cancelled due to COVID-19, so we began to meet over Zoom.

To be honest, we all were a bit skeptical about the purpose and expectation of our meetings—we didn't even have a name for the group! But as we met and began to express our feelings, we began to listen to each other and gain a respect for each other's opinions. It was a shared journey of faith with no clear purpose. And then the killing of George Floyd exploded in American headlines and soon thereafter, around the world. The need for better race relations was suddenly at the forefront of American and church politics. Who would have known that but God? We had confirmation that God had called us together. It was a humbling realization.

We continued to meet but we wanted to do more. We had to be part of the solution, so we wrote a letter to our church leaders. Mark and his fellow deacon co-authored it and it was impactful to those in the group. I include the first three paragraphs here.

....

An Open Letter to Seventh-day Adventists

Dear Seventh-day Adventists,

We have been hiding in the crowd long enough. The years of complacency and inattention have devolved into apathy. Our deafening silence has left a void where urgency and expectancy should have been our burden for the souls of all people. Rather than standing on God's word as our firm foundation to ac-

knowledge social ills that plague many believers, and being buoyed above the din of the masses, we set it aside—yet stood close enough to wag it at others. We blended in with the masses and are now indistinct and unrecognizable. Says the Lord, "Cry aloud, spare not, lift up thy voice like a trumpet, and shew my people their transgression, and the house of Jacob their sins." (Isaiah 58:1)

Seventh-day Adventists, what we have done wrong is that we acted as though we were unacquainted with good and evil, the notions of fairness and justice, the recognition of the common struggles of men and women attempting to live as though they are truly equal. So, like Paul, when Peter chose not to associate with the Gentiles who had come into the faith, we must be "withstood to the face, because [we are] to be blamed." (Galatians 2:11) Seventh-day Adventist, you are "Peter" if, to you, "the Gentiles" are identified by the color of their skin. Seventh-day Adventist, you are "Peter" if, to you, "the Gentiles" are those who believe the process of sanctification is the only means for social, judicial or other reforms.

Are we not all created in His image, and given "the right to become children of God"? (John 1:12, NIV) If so, then why are we such a dysfunctional family? Do we even see the hope of brotherhood that God created and to which we are joined by our common humanity, and red blood?

....

The rest of the letter appealed to our fellow church members to remember our past, the Adventist heritage and to embrace the future that God has promised His church.

Josue took the letter to the General Conference of Seventh-day Adventist and it was well received. Pastor Jerry Page, who is White, took our message to heart and asked to meet with us. He met with us on Zoom for our third monthly meeting. Let me say here that it's amazing to see God perform miracles in real time. That's what we were witnessing. Later, Jerry invited Pastor Anthony Kent, who is also White, to our fifth meeting. Our group was growing and becoming more inclusive and our conversations were candid yet tactful. Honestly, there were some tense moments in our meetings but we were truthful and not a condemning word was spoken. God gave us a name for our group: Men of Prayer and Purpose (MOPAP). That meeting was only the beginning; the story is far from over and it is interwoven into my story.

Purpose in Adversity

My story continued as I sat at my desk in my home office on a late spring Sabbath morning. I had just opened the email from LabCorp with my most recent prostate specific antigen (PSA) test results. My PSA had gone up ever so slightly, and that was not the news I expected nor wanted to hear. My number had been below zero for 18 months. I wondered, *why now?* That was June of 2021 and I knew I was in for another round of treatment. I prayed and asked God what it all meant. I had learned so much through my surgery and recovery. I had grown closer to God and began to trust Him in a way I never had before. I was living a miracle, unfolding with me in it. My resolve was simple: I would not doubt Him. I had a Zoom meeting that day with MOPAP. Although I wanted to, I would not share the news with them, at least not yet. I would not let my wife or family know either. I needed to collect my emotions and see what the treatment options were. I prayed for healing, strength, and courage.

A few days went by, and I was thinking how to tell my wife when a familiar voice whispered to me, "I am so sorry that you have to go through this." I knew my heavenly Father's voice. I was familiar with His assuring tone, but I wasn't certain what He meant. I would learn in due time. I emailed Dr. Hwang, and he responded with a referral. I told Cassandra. She was noticeably shaken, but she handled the news well. We decided not to tell the rest of the family until we had met with the doctor.

Our initial meeting with Dr. Pamela Randolph-Jackson, a radiology on-cologist, was in July. When Cassandra and I went to meet with her, we ran into a very old friend and classmate, Joyce Smith. She worked for the radiology department at Washington Hospital Center, and it was her last day before retirement! We all embraced and seeing her there calmed my nerves. We took it as a sign from God.

Dr. Randolph-Jackson was personable and took time to explain the rec-ommended treatment options based on national medical standards. It was quite a bit of information, and we had a lot of questions. She answered them one by one and explained the radiation protocol. I would need to take daily sessions of radiation; a total of 30 in all. I looked at my wife, and she looked at me. We both sighed. In addition, hormone therapy might be necessary. Pamela gave me a referral for her associate.

I had a lot to consider and a lot to pray about. We told our family, and I shared the news with MOPAP and some of my elders. Some of them took it hard which made me uneasy. One of our church elders had recently died from cancer and another, Jude Patrick, was currently in treatment for breast cancer. Jude and I had become close as we shared the ups and downs of our treatments. In fact, I was present when the Capitol Hill el-ders and Pastor Peeler anointed her at the church office building. I prayed for her continually.

I started treatment in late August, and Cassandra went with me on the first day. I was glad she was with me. It reminded me of Aunt Annie Mae and all those trips to the doctor I made with her as a child. As I recall, that was 30 trips in all. I was a grown man now, but some of those fears I had as a child I still carried with me as an adult.

The treatments were difficult because the radiation was in a sensitive part of the body. My bladder had to be full, and my bowel had to be empty. That was a difficult balance to get right. Daily laxatives were required to empty the bowel and drinking the right amount of water was often hit

or miss. Fortunately, I had others going through the same process as me.
Some of the guys would have suffered in silence, but I made it a point to
talk to the men who were with me. After a while, we knew each other's
names and situations. We exchanged treatment tips and encouraged one
another. Many of us really needed that.

Mr. Crayton was the oldest among us and had retired from the Secret Service. Winston was an electrician who had lived in Fort Washington. His
nephew was a Seventh-day Adventist minister. Larry, Omar, and Jackson
had the most difficulty with the treatment protocol. Larry and Jackson
would be there for hours sometimes trying to get treatment. Omar had to
discontinue treatment for a time due to bad side effects. Ronnie and Ward
were the last to start treatment—the former was talkative; the latter was
not. Sometimes we would all be in the waiting room, our legs twitching,
trying to hold our water as best we could. To see all these old men in obvious distress, holding their bladders, would have been funny in another
circumstance, but the treatment began to wear on each of us. I began to
feel like I could not complete the treatment. Treatment days 17 and 18
were bad days for me on the radiation table, and it weighed on me. Then I
met with my doctor only to be told that I was scheduled for 37 treatments
and not 30. How had I made that mistake? It wasn't just me—Cassandra
had heard the same thing.

Later, I was at home looking in the mirror and thinking, *Lord, I cannot
do this. I want to stop. How can I stop?* Then I understood what He had
whispered to me those months before. Sometimes we cannot stop. Sometimes we must go through the valley even if it leads to death. Jeremiah the
prophet understood:

> So they took Jeremiah and put him into the cistern of Malkijah, the
> king's son, which was in the courtyard of the guard. They lowered Jer-

emiah by ropes into the cistern; it had no water in it, only mud, and Jeremiah sank down into the mud.

—*Jeremiah 38:6 NIV*

I imagined how Jeremiah must have felt. I was in a spot up to my neck in mud. I was in God's will and I was confident of that, but I was restricted by circumstances and I could not free myself. I had to trust God. Prayer takes on a new reality in times like those. So, I prayed and I waited for God to answer. This was my Jeremiah moment, and it was difficult.

The next day, as Winston and I waited in the treatment room, I confided in him. "Man, I don't think I can do this. I don't know if I can complete my treatment!"

With a calm serenity, Winston responded, "Sure, Nate, you can do it."

I looked at Winston, knowing that his words of encouragement, although spoken by him, were from my heavenly Father. I knew he was right and I felt renewed. My attitude changed. "Attitude Matters" became my slogan for the remainder of my treatment. I settled down into a routine, determined to complete all my treatments.

On the 8th of October the Men of Prayer and Purpose was scheduled to do our first annual Reconciliation Dinner. The dinner was inspired by an event held right after the American Civil War where Whites and Blacks, some former slaves and some former slave owners, came together as equals to break bread. It was through Terrell's efforts that the event was made possible. As a notable former head chef he'd heard about the event and thought it would be in perfect accord with our group. Plans and preparations were made and the dinner was held at Capitol Hill Church in the reception area.

The weather had been beautiful and although I had radiation treatment that day, I felt wonderful. Although our original group had only seven members, there were 22 men there that night in attendance. The group was diverse with Blacks, Whites, Hispanic, and East Indian men present. Wow, what a great start! We knew it was God in our midst and we relished every moment we spent together. We laughed, we gave testimonies, we prayed, we ate and finally we made commitments to each other to continue what we had started, rather what God had started. I had seen God perform another miracle and I looked forward to my last week of treatment.

I counted down the days as I made the trek through traffic to the hospital. I brought *Steps to Christ* books and passed them out to patients and staff alike. God is faithful. My side effects were minimal and I had no bleeding or skin peeling. That was another miracle, and it was God answering my prayers. But it wasn't just my most recent prayers He had answered.

Childhood and adolescent prayers had been answered too. Prayers to overcome fear, prayers for understanding, and prayers for spiritual healing were part of the gift of this trial. The years that the locusts had consumed were restored. This trial made me focus all of my attention on God. I fasted from television, social media, and processed sweets for the duration of treatment, which was 53 days in all. It was not as hard as I had feared. In fact, I was grateful as my mind became sharp and the distractions in my life faded into the insignificance that was their rightful place.

I had also prayed to God to prepare me for the time of trouble coming upon the world. I had spent so much time thinking about what could happen or what would happen that I forgot something I learned as a child; "He's got the whole world in His hands." I was afraid of the future, as if God doesn't own the future. Every atom, every molecule, belongs to and is controlled by our heavenly Father. Just as He brought me through my cancer trial, He will bring me through whatever else I may face. Was it worth it, to gain that understanding and faith? Yes, it was!

On the last day of cancer treatment, it is customary to "ring the bell." I am not sure how the tradition started, but when radiation or chemotherapy treatments have been successfully completed, the patient rings the bell. That treatment bell was right outside the radiation room door at Washington Hospital Center.

As I lifted myself off the radiation table and put on my hospital gown, I wasn't concerned about my overfull bladder. I would have normally rushed to the restroom in the waiting area, but not that day. I stepped out with a placard that my daughter Xavian had helped me make. The placard was simple. It was a blue cancer ribbon on a white background with the text *Psalm 23* painted in the hoop portion. I held it up with one hand and rang the bell with my other. I rang the bell with giddy enthusiasm as Rima, the radiology technician, took my photo. We hugged and wished each other the best. That was that.

Just as He had promised, God had walked with me through the valley. He never breaks a promise.

> God is not a man, that he should lie; neither the son of man, that he should repent: hath he said, and shall he not do it? or hath he spoken, and shall he not make it good?
>
> —*Numbers 23:19 KJV*

Afterword

A s I come to the close of this first installment of this series, the writing has been a journey of trust. Joshua 1:9, as well as so many other Bible verses, has lifted me above my fears. Walking by faith also requires patience and keeping our eyes fixed on Christ in every storm. Writing has cemented for me the belief that I'm in His will and that the message in these pages must be told with force and clarity. I welcome the call.

The second installment of *My Story, His Glory* shares what I have learned about the gospel as God has revealed it to me though His Word, the Bible, by His Spirit, and through my experience. The inspired understanding of the Bible, God's Word, has been indispensable in my journey. The same can be said for the influence of the Holy Spirit. Most Christians would probably say the same thing about their personal journeys. As I reflect, I now understand that my each and every experience has benefited me. God has used them in my sanctification walk. His love has shielded me and protected me. Whenever I needed Him, He was always there. That's true in every instance.

> And we know that all things work together for good to them that love God, to them who are the called according to his purpose.
>
> For whom he did foreknow, he also did predestinate to be conformed to the image of his Son, that he might be the firstborn among many brethren.
>
> Moreover whom he did predestinate, them he also called: and whom he called, them he also justified: and whom he justified, them he also glorified.
>
> —*Romans 8:28-30 NKJV*

I was shown that none of my experiences were by accident or chance. They were all acts of providence guided by a loving Father and His benevolent hand. Thank you, Father! That is special, but it is not unique. Each person in God's creation can understand what I have come to know—that God, in His love has ordered my steps to bring about my salvation. He has done the same for you. Through this series, *Understanding the Angels of Revelation*, it is my purpose to share with you what God has shared with me—the certainty that Christ's return is imminent.

I also came to understand that the Bible is not a mere collection of stories told by men and women long dead, in situations irrelevant to me today.

The Bible is a living and breathing instrument used by the Divine Author to create new stories in every man and woman alive today. That includes you. You are part of Christ's "autobiography," just as were Moses, Peter, John, Paul, David, Ruth and Ester. He is the God of the living and we are alive in Him.

What does that really mean? It means that the plan of salvation is fitted specifically, especially for you! Your every foible and flaw, every defect of DNA and every contaminant of character is covered by Jesus' blood. Every fall and misstep, every experience is under the blood. Christ cares for you supremely. It's amazing when you contemplate it.

I have discussed my Red Sea experience, my Jordan River experience, and my Job experience. I have mentioned my Jacob experience, my Jeremiah, and my Joel experiences. Although separated by eons, the Bible writer's experiences, mine, and yours are part of the same cloth and pattern. You should understand that and take it to heart. It is important that you bring this perspective with you as we continue our journey together. Remember that you are an integral part of this grand autobiography.

Additionally, Book 2 will explain the great controversy between Christ and Satan in a way that you will understand and you will see how you are a central part of it. In the great controversy, there are no casual observers and no neutral parties. We will explain the landmarks of biblical prophecy by an exposition of the Sanctuary and what it reveals to us. We will delve deeply into the mysteries of life and ask questions that have befuddled many. The origin of sin and suffering, the plan of salvation, its beginning and ending, will all be explored and explained. When we study the Word of God, the maelstrom of deceptions and the cacophony of lies posited by the enemy will be exposed, and the darkness in our lives will be scattered.

The final installment, Book 3 explains end time prophecy as it explodes around us in events, headlines, and in our individual lives. We will bring into focus what is truth and what is deception. In Matthew 24, Jesus warned us multiple times not to be deceived. Deception then is the zeit-geist of our age. The only thing that can counteract it is what the Apostle Peter called the "present truth," and it has never been more important to understand than now.

> Wherefore I will not be negligent to put you always in remembrance of these things, though ye know them, and be established in the present truth.
>
> —*2 Peter 1:12 KJV*

Christ's warning and Peter's admonition is the theme of Book 3. The gravity of our times and the stakes involved cannot be overstated. Indeed, eternity lies in the balance—mine and yours. You need to know what awaits us, our collective future, and it's our mission to help you understand. We will bring these things to remembrance and establish you firmly in the present truth.

In these last days we can expect the enemy to pull out all the stops. He has practiced his craft of deception for nearly 6,000 years and he has honed it to perfection. We will expose what he has done and what his plans are. Remember, the conflict has raged for millennia and its final scenes of trauma, we cannot imagine. Still, God's elect has the promise that God's grace is sufficient. We will be tested in a way no generation before us has. Let us be prepared.

> Take no part in the worthless deeds of evil and darkness; instead, expose them. It is shameful even to talk about the things that ungodly people do in secret. But their evil intentions will be exposed when the light shines on them, for the light makes everything visible. This

is why it is said, "Awake, O sleeper, rise up from the dead, and Christ will give you light.

—*Ephesians 5:11-14 NLT)*

Exercises

H*uman experiences, although separated by time and* geography, are amazingly similar. Consequently, our problems and their solutions are also similar to those of others. I am convinced that there is a right method to resolving any life problem. The exercises at the end of each chapter are designed to help you discover for yourself these biblically sound and proven methods.

Just reading the contents of this book without applying the concepts directly to your life situation is unlikely to change or transform your situation. So, I challenge you to complete the exercises for each chapter. Complete the exercises after first reading the section or after reading the whole book and then address the activities section by section. Whatever way you choose, by all means Complete the exercises!

Introduction Exercises

1. Recall the very first time you remember being aware of God's presence. Where were you? What were you doing? Did you know it was God? When you think about that time now, how do you feel?

2. Were there any difficult situations going on in your life that diminished or colored that experience? What were they? Were they resolved or do they still fester? How do you feel about them now?

3. Is what you experienced then the same thing(s) you are still struggling with now? How so? What changed? When did it change?

4. Cite a Scripture, quote, poem or writing for exercises 1, 2, and 3 and reflect on what it means to you now. Write it down and then share it with a friend.

Chapter 1 Exercises

1. What were the nuclear forces in your early life—the situations that shaped your emotions and personality? For example, were you an only child or did you come from a broken home? Think of the experiences that might have fractured your youth. How did they affect your view of the people around you, your community, and the world?

2. Do you see any relation to how you felt then and how you live/feel now?

3. What emotions characterize that time best for you? Joy, depression, fear, or confusion? If it wasn't one of those, what was it?

4. Do those feelings still linger in your present behavior toward the world? Is there a song, writing, movie, or a Scripture that you

related to them? Reflect on what it means to you now. Write it down and then share it with a friend you knew at that time in your life. What do they think about what you shared?

Chapter 2 Exercises

1. What were the early religious influences in your life? Were they your family or friends? Are they part of your life now? Why or why not?

2. What is the most important issue in your life now? Does your religion/belief system resolve or complicate it?

3. Does your religion/belief system help or hurt your human relationships? Reflect on what caused the situation and what you can do to change the situation. Is there a Scripture or text that is helpful?

Chapter 3 Exercises

1. Times of transition like young adulthood can be difficult. In navigating career choices, selecting a life partner, and deciding on where to live are all challenges. How did you manage your transitions?

2. In a short reflective piece (one page or less) describe those challenges, how you managed them, and with whose help.

Chapter 4 Exercises

Hurt, pain, suffering, and death are real. Answer the following questions in writing and then reflect on them.

1. When you witness or experience what you consider injustice in the world around you, how do you address it?

2. What is your reaction to that injustice? Does it make you feel angry, helpless, or hopeless? What do you feel?

3. Who do you blame for what you see happening?

4. Do you feel that there is any real hope to finding a solution?

Chapter 5 Exercises

American societal beliefs and norms vary greatly. Take time to reflect upon and respond in writing to the following questions.

1. Does your family history and religion affect your views of right and wrong and is that belief biased toward and based on race? Is this bias unconscious?

2. Are our culture's norms and laws favorable to the people group you identify with and should it be that way?

3. Depending on your response to number two, what are you willing to do to change things for the better?

4. Is the change you seek something that God wants or requires?

Chapter 6 Exercises

Life changing health events are often beyond our control. When they happen, how do you first respond?

1. Do you become paralyzed with fear?

2. Are you overcome with depression and have no hope?

3. What people do you call on for help?

4. Is your religion personal during those times and is it a source of help?

Chapter 7 Exercises

Crisis in our world often has a domino effect impacting our country, our culture, and ourselves. Give serious thought to how various crisis have affected you in the past. Also, as you reflect on that question, think about why the Bible tells us that there is only one God and one way to Him, and that is through Jesus Christ.

How and why are these two apparently disparate things connected? Write your thoughts down and try to limit it to one page.

Chapter 8 Exercises

To make changes in one's life is rarely easy. Think about the changes you decided to make in your life; reflect and write down your responses to the following questions.

1. What prompted the change?

2. Why was the change necessary?

3. Did you speak to anyone about making the change?

4. Was God a consideration for you?

Chapter 9 Exercises

Reflect on the ups and downs, the course of your life, and answer the following questions. Be thorough.

1. Have you discovered the reason you are here?

2. Does your life have the meaning and purpose you intended it to have?

3. If it does or doesn't, why?

4. Is this life all there is or is there an eternity in the hereafter?

5. What is your destiny?

Afterword Exercises

God wants you to be informed and prepared for the dramatic changes coming upon us. Social unrest, climate catastrophes, famines, wars and pestilences are all end time events predicted in Scripture. The next two installments of this series are designed to help you prepare. Complete the following exercises in anticipation of those changes.

The longest Bible date prophecy stretches 2,300 years and ends in the modern era. God gave us that prophecy Himself. I discuss this in great detail in Book 2.

If you've seen the movie *The Godfather* you have a glimpse into the machinations of evil. The scene where the mob bosses get together at a table to agree on how and to what extent they will distribute drugs to different ethnic groups is agreed upon. Satan and his "mob bosses" did the very same thing. Only their meeting was real. It included every ethnic group on planet earth, and it happened in the 1700s.

They were dealing something more dangerous than drugs—they were distributing "end time deceptions." In order to win people over and to create havoc in the world and turmoil in individual lives, Satan had to do three things:

1. Convince people that he, Satan and his angels do not really exist.

2. Find a way to get total control of people's minds through the power of suggestion and hypnotism (He would use science and technology to accomplish this.).

3. Create a way to destroy the Bible without burning it.

    a. Does what I've shared about Satan's plans seem far-fetched to you? Why?

    b. Do you know what hypnotism is and how it is done?

    c. Why doesn't the devil want you believe that he exists?

    d. Does the theory of evolution effectively "burn" the Bible? How?

Endnotes

1   Martin Luther King Jr., "Remaining Awake Through a Great Revolution" speech
    delivered at the National Cathedral, Washington, D.C., March 31, 1968, Caribbean
    National Weekly, accessed August 24, 2022, https://www.caribbeannationalweekly.
    com/caribbean-breaking-news-featured/mlk-jr-remaining-awake-revolution/.

2   W. E. B. DuBois, *The Souls of Black Folk* (Chicago: A.C. McClurg & Co., 1903).

3   Ernest Hemingway, *The Sun Also Rises* (New York: Scribner's, 1926).

4   Malcolm X, *The Autobiography of Malcolm X* (New York: Grove Press, 1965).

5   Anthony Browder *Nile Valley Contributions to Civilization* (Washington, D.C.:
    Institute of Karmic Guidance, 1992).

6   "The Rodney King Affair," L.A. Times, March 24, 1991, https://www.latimes.com/
    archives/la-xpm-1991-03-24-me-1422-story.html.

7   Carter G. Woodson, *The Mis-Education of the Negro* (Washington, D.C.: The
    Associated Publishers, 1933).

8   "Alfredo Bowman," Black History Wiki, accessed September 15, 2022, https://black-
    history.fandom.com/wiki/Alfredo_Bowman.

9   Richard B. Schmitt, Kim Christensen, E. Scott, Reckard, "400 Charged as U.S.
    Cracks Down on Mortgage Fraud," L.A. Times, June 20, 2008, https://www.latimes.
    com/archives/la-xpm-2008-jun-20-fi-mortgage20-story.html.

10 "Mortgage Fraud Report 2008," FBI, accessed September 15, 2022, https://www.fbi. gov/stats-services/publications/mortgage-fraud-2008.

11 Ellen G. White, *The Desire of Ages* (Washington, D.C.: Review and Herald Publishing Association, 1898), 256.

12 Ellen G. White, *Testimonies for the Church*, vol. 5 (Washington, D.C.: Review and Herald Publishing Association, 1889), 293.

13 Ellen G. White, *Christ's Object Lessons* (Battle Creek: Review and Herald Pub. Co., 1900), 65-66.

Keep in Touch

Find out more about my story and get resources to understand the Bible and what is happening in the world now.

BE PREPARED! 🌐 **HISGLORYPUBLISHING.COM**

Book Nathaniel X. Arnold for speaking events by contacting His Glory Publishing, LLC at *contact@hisglorypublishing.com*

Join our email list and receive exclusive weekly blog articles.

If you would like to join our Men of Prayer and Purpose Bible discussion group, email us at: *menofprayerandpurpose@gmail.com*

For special discounts or bulk purchases, contact us at: *contact@hisglorypublishing.com*

Thank You For Reading!

If you enjoyed My Story, His Glory, please leave a review on Goodreads or on the retailer site where you purchased the book.

Sign up for Book 2 at our website

WWW.HISGLORYPUBLISHING.COM

CPSIA information can be obtained
at www.ICGtesting.com
Printed in the USA
BVHW050842090323
660078BV00014B/281/J